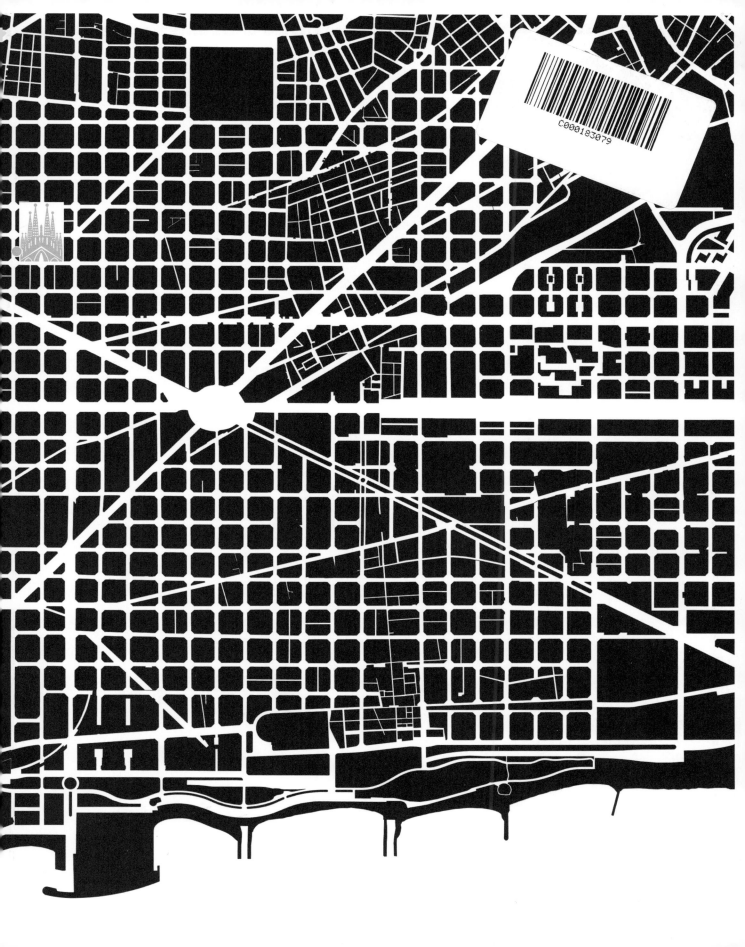

BARCELONA

CULT RECIPES

STEPHAN MITSCH
PHOTOS BY ARNOLD PÖSCHL

BARCELONA
CULT RECIPES

MURDOCH BOOKS
SYDNEY · LONDON

CONTENTS

THERE IS NO PARADISE. GOD LIVES HERE!

Barcelona, this old yet eternally young city, is one of only a few in the world that has successfully reinvented itself. The city underwent major refurbishment for the Olympic Games in 1992, when it was given a new public transport system, a new airport and even completely new suburbs. Since then, it has slowly but surely become a top destination for tourists from all over the world. And they're right: Barcelona is definitely worth a visit, for so much more than sightseeing.

Barcelona, the capital of the Spanish region of Catalonia, has always attracted lots of people. Migrants from poorer areas of Spain, including the regions of Andalusia, Extremadura and Galicia, came as early as the 19th century in search of a better life. They brought not only their customs from their native regions but also their recipes. No need to deprive yourself! This is how Barcelonian cuisine came to incorporate many different influences: gazpacho from Andalusia, paella from Valencia, marmitako from the Basque country and many other dishes. Later, migrants from the Near, Middle and Far East, from Africa and from South and Central America brought even more colour to the culinary potpourri that is this city. Cassava, plantains, sweet potatoes, mung beans, ginger, curry and soy sauce have all become fixtures in Barcelonian cuisine, which is a true *cocina de fusión*.

I've never come across any other city that makes it so easy to spoil yourself with truly amazing food at such reasonable prices. The Mediterranean Sea is right at the city's doorstep, and the surrounding regions are veritable treasure troves of culinary delights. The almost limitless selection of fish and seafood in *La boquería*, Barcelona's best-known market, invites you to explore the city's rich food culture. El Prat de Llobregat, the delta of the Llobregat river south-west of Barcelona, is the city's kitchen garden, where delicious *calçots* (spring onions/scallions) and cabbages are grown in winter and fantastic artichokes and broad beans in spring. Farmers cultivate a huge variety of vegetables here throughout the year, including chickpeas, tomatoes, eggplant (aubergine) and various types of fruit. Catalans are obsessive about

mushrooms and cook with vast amounts of them in autumn. This is when red pine mushrooms, chanterelles and Caesar's mushrooms feature prominently on the menus of local restaurants. Traditional Spanish cuisine also uses a lot of rice, not only in the famous paella, and this is also true for Barcelona. Luckily there is a huge rice-growing region a little further south of the city, near Tortosa in the Ebro delta.

Spaniards also love pasta. Filled, large pasta tubes called *canelones* are a traditional Christmas dish, and *escudella i carn d'olla*, the region's famous meat and pasta stew, is a must on major holidays. *Fideos*, a type of thin, short noodles, are very important, too; these are usually cooked together with seafood, mushrooms, vegetables or poultry in the same stock.

Poultry is, of course, very important in traditional Catalan cooking. Chickens, ducks, quail, delectable pheasants and *perdices*, which are quite similar to partridges, are cooked throughout the year according to a seemingly endless variety of recipes. Naturally, meat also plays a major role in Spanish cuisine: there is rabbit, lamb and beef (excellent beef is produced in the neighbouring region around Girona) and, above all, pork. Venison makes its way into Catalan pots and pans in autumn, and 'poor man's meat', that is, snails, also deserve a mention.

One of the outstanding features of Catalan cuisine is dishes that fuse ingredients sourced from the sea and the land (*mar i muntanya*), in combinations that often seem almost outlandish to non-locals. There is bean soup with mussels, rabbit with prawns (shrimp) or chicken with fish and seafood, to name just a few.

Now a few words on dining culture: Spaniards have very frugal breakfasts, often consisting of no more than a cup of coffee at home. On their way to work they might then have a *bocadillo*, that is, a small roll, or a *cruasán*. Simply try to pronounce this – and yes, it is indeed a croissant! If people get hungry before lunch, they can always snack on a few tapas in the late morning, as Spaniards only have lunch from about 2 pm. In the late afternoon, they might then have a few more tapas with a *vermut* or a *caña*, that is, a draught beer. People usually do not come home from work until late, so dinner is also a late affair. Restaurants open at about 8.30 pm at the earliest, and dinner is generally quite rich, especially on weekends. The culinary highlights described below are well worth your attention during a stroll through Barcelona – everything else you'll find in your travel guide!

In the old quarter of El Born/La Ribera you'll find some palaces that are well worth a visit, but most importantly this quarter is home to the Mercat de Santa Caterina, which was fully refurbished a few years ago and fitted with a colourful new roof. Here, you'll find a number of interesting bars and restaurants, for example the 'Cuines Santa Caterina' inside the market. The Gothic quarter of El Raval is right next to Las Ramblas in the city centre. This is where Barcelona's high society moved to between the 17th and 19th centuries in an attempt to escape the dark and narrow lanes of the 'old' part of the city, and this is where you'll find, above all, the world-famous *La boquería* or Mercat de Sant Josep. Sadly, the market has been losing some of its authentic appeal due to a steady stream of tourists, and these days many stalls sell fancy colourful fruit cocktails rather than fruit and vegetables.

However, if you are lucky enough to find a seat in the 'El Quim de la Boquería' or in the 'Pinotxo', you'll be spoiled with authentic dishes. Even Raval still has some good restaurants, for example the stunningly beautiful 'Fonda España' in the Hotel España or the 'Ca l'Isidre', a true bastion of traditional Catalan cuisine. The old, recently re-opened brewery Moritz in the quarter of Sant Antoni serves beer on tap. The quarter of Eixample ('extension'), which was built as recently as the turn of the 20th century, also has a wealth of interesting restaurants, as do the quarters of Gràcia, Sant Gervasi and Sarrià. I'll only mention three examples: 'Tragaluz', 'Osmosis' and 'Etapes', but there are plenty more, and shops in the little side streets sell anything and everything to do with food and cooking. If you love fish and seafood, you may want to head for the restaurants of Barceloneta, which was the fishermen's quarter a long time ago. Newer quarters such as Poblenou, which was built for the Olympic Games, or 22@, also have a great restaurant culture. The latter is home to the ESHOB – the Barcelona School of Culinary Arts and Gastronomy.

The Catalan master chef Ferran Adrià revolutionised the international culinary world with his ground-breaking creations, and his style of molecular cooking has also had a clear influence on Barcelonian cuisine. His cuisine, which is everything but traditional and combines aromas, colours and textures to appeal to all senses, demonstrates that food and eating can be so much more than merely taking in nutrients. Catalan cuisine, which is widely known for fusing traditional and new elements in many wonderful ways, for transforming conventional ingredients with outstanding creativity and for preserving traditional cooking methods, has also opened up to Ferran Adrià's ideas.

All of these influences have created one of the tastiest cuisines in all of Europe. I'll introduce the dishes under their traditional Catalan and Spanish names as well as with an English translation. Some dishes are only known under their Catalan or Spanish names, though.

So, a few words about myself. How did I end up in Barcelona? That's a long story, but I'll make it short. When I was a child, I was 'transplanted' from Frisia in northern Germany to Ethiopia. I later moved back to Germany, to Düsseldorf, then to Schwetzingen and Frankfurt. I first visited Barcelona a long time before anyone in Germany knew much about the fabulous Catalan cuisine, about 25 years ago. At the time, I didn't try much beyond paella, *gambas al ajillo*, *patatas bravas* and deep-fried fish. But about 15 years ago, I settled in Barcelona. I'm almost pathologically curious and I have absorbed as much as possible of the Catalan lifestyle, culture and language, including the unique local cuisine. Today I'm sure that there is no paradise. God lives here!

A stroll through the narrow lanes in Barcelona's old town helps work up an appetite and is a veritable invitation to indulge in the city's culinary delights.

Once upon a time, tapas was nothing more than a slice of ham or cured meat that was placed on top of a wine glass, mainly in southern Spain, to prevent flies from falling into the wine.

The Spanish word *tapa* means simply 'lid'. But then these little morsels evolved in the most creative of ways. Many dishes that we now know as tapas, for example croquettes or Russian salad, originated as inventive and delicious ways of using up leftovers from the day before. Now that tapas have become a trendy gourmet experience, they are always freshly prepared. These days, you'll find an enormous selection of tapas on offer, and there are tapas bars and even specialised tapas restaurants in Barcelona and elsewhere.

TAPAS

CROQUETES
CROQUETAS
CROQUETTES

Spanish croquettes are very different from what are commonly know as croquettes elsewhere. The first written record of Iberian croquettes goes back to the French author Alexandre Dumas, who enjoyed them during his travels in Spain. Spanish croquettes are based on a relatively firm béchamel sauce that is combined with other ingredients. There are innumerable varieties, but the general preparation always follows the same rules.

1. The béchamel sauce base must be quite firm.

2. The croquettes should all be about the same size, but the shape is irrelevant. The dough should be cold, straight out of a refrigerator, and the croquettes are best shaped using an ice cream scoop.

3. The crumbing step is particularly important: whisk the egg well. For best results, always use freshly crumbed stale bread.

4. Use a small rather than a large pan for deep-frying to ensure that the croquettes are fully immersed in hot oil and cannot break or burst open. Oil for deep-frying has the right temperature if tiny bubbles rise when you drop a trial croquette into the oil. Never try to deep-fry too many croquettes at once!

5. Uncooked croquettes can be frozen and cooked fresh at a later time. Make sure you defrost them fully before deep-frying: there's nothing worse than croquettes that look beautifully golden on the outside but are still frozen and raw inside.

CROQUETES AMB CHORIZO
CROQUETAS CON CHORIZO
CROQUETTES WITH CHORIZO

Here are three traditional variations of plain croquettes.

Makes 40 small croquettes | **Preparation:** 45 minutes
Chilling time: 12 hours, best overnight | **Deep-frying time:** 25–30 minutes

INGREDIENTS

For the croquettes

200 g (7 oz) chorizo

For the béchamel base

100 g (3½ oz) butter
100 g (3½ oz) plain (all-purpose)
    flour
1 litre (35 fl oz) full-cream milk
Freshly ground nutmeg

For the coating

2–3 eggs
Breadcrumbs

Also

Plenty of olive oil for deep-frying

PREPARE THE DOUGH

Remove the skin from the chorizo and chop the sausage meat finely. Heat a dry frying pan over medium heat. Fry the chopped chorizo for a few minutes, stirring. Remove from the pan and drain on paper towel.

Melt the butter in a large saucepan over medium heat. Add and sweat the flour, stirring. Be careful not to let it burn. Gradually add the milk, whisking continuously to prevent lumps from forming. Season with salt, freshly ground black pepper and nutmeg. Continue to simmer for another 15 minutes to thicken.

Add the flavouring ingredients, in this case the chorizo, and simmer for another 5 minutes. Transfer the mixture to a bowl. Cover with plastic wrap and refrigerate for several hours, ideally overnight, to allow the mixture to firm up.

SHAPE THE CROQUETTES

Whisk the eggs in a shallow bowl. Transfer the breadcrumbs to a deep plate. Use an ice cream scoop to divide the béchamel mixture into balls of equal size. Shape round or oval croquettes. Dip and turn the croquettes first in the egg, then in the breadcrumbs. Deep-fry in the hot oil, then drain on paper towel.

VARIATIONS

Croquettes are the perfect base for many different flavourings and ingredients, including fish (tuna or bacalao/salt cod), seafood, cheese, vegetables and more. Avoid adding too many ingredients to any particular type of croquettes, or they may fall apart.

CROQUETES AMB CEPS
CROQUETAS DE SETAS
CROQUETTES WITH MUSHROOMS

INGREDIENTS
Butter for sautéing

1–2 onions, finely chopped

200 g (7 oz) porcini or mixed mushrooms, finely diced

100 ml (3½ fl oz) robust white wine

1 tablespoon curly parsley, chopped

Melt the butter in a frying pan over medium heat. Add the onions and sauté until golden brown. Add the mushrooms, increase the heat to high and fry. Season the mixture with salt and freshly ground black pepper and deglaze with the white wine. Simmer to reduce.

Remove the mushroom mixture from the pan and drain in a sieve or on paper towel. Mix in the parsley and continue as in the recipe on page 16.

CROQUETES DE POLLO
CROQUETAS DE POLLO
CROQUETTES WITH CHICKEN

INGREDIENTS
Butter for sautéing

2 onions, finely chopped

250 g (9 oz) skinless chicken breast fillet, finely diced

Melt the butter in a frying pan over medium heat. Add the onions and sauté until golden brown. Add the chicken and sauté for a few minutes, stirring occasionally, then season to taste with salt and freshly ground white pepper.

Remove the chicken mixture from the pan and drain in a sieve or on paper towel. Continue as in the recipe on page 16.

CROQUETES CASERAS DE ESPINACS

CROQUETAS CASERAS DE ESPINACAS
CROQUETTES WITH SPINACH

In another version, the béchamel sauce is made using the flavouring ingredient.

Makes 40 small croquettes | **Preparation:** 45 minutes
Chilling time: 12 hours, best overnight | **Deep-frying time:** 25–30 minutes

INGREDIENTS

For the croquettes

200 g (7 oz) frozen English spinach
1 pinch salt
80 g (2¾ oz) butter
2 tablespoons plain (all-purpose) flour
400 ml (14 fl oz) milk
50 g (1¾ oz) blue-vein cheese, crumbled

For the coating

2–3 eggs
Breadcrumbs

Also

Plenty of olive oil for deep-frying

PREPARATION

Cook the spinach in a little salted water for 5 minutes. Strain through a sieve, drain well and squeeze out the excess water. Melt the butter in a frying pan over medium heat. Add the spinach and sauté briefly. Stir in the flour. Gradually add the milk, stirring constantly until the mixture thickens to a creamy, green béchamel sauce. Take the pan off the heat and fold the crumbled cheese into the hot sauce until it has melted. Refrigerate for 12 hours. Shape into croquettes, crumb and deep-fry (see page 16).

CROQUETES AMB CECINA
CROQUETAS CON CECINA
CROQUETTES WITH CECINA AND LEEKS

INGREDIENTS

Butter for sautéing

1 small leek, finely sliced

150 g (5½ oz) cecina (air-dried beef), finely chopped

Melt the butter in a frying pan over medium heat. Add the leek and sauté until golden brown. Add the cecina or air-dried beef. Continue to sauté for a few minutes, stirring occasionally, then season to taste with salt and freshly ground black pepper. Remove the beef mixture from the pan and drain in a sieve or on paper towel. Continue as in the recipe on page 16.

PAN AMB TOMAQUET
PAN CON TOMATE
BREAD WITH TOMATO

This is one of the classics of Catalan cuisine that everyone knows. Barcelonian restaurants often serve this simple dish automatically as a starter. As with so many other dishes of Catalan and Spanish cuisine, it originated as typical peasant food. Stale slices of white bread were not thrown away, but rather rubbed with half a tomacó, *an ancient variety of tomato with a hard skin that keeps the fruit inside fresh for months. Sometime the bread was also rubbed with a garlic clove. It was then drizzled with olive oil and salt before serving. Traditionally,* pan amb tomaquet *was prepared with a slice of toasted or roasted* pan de pagès, *a type of rustic white bread.*

Preparation: 10 minutes

INGREDIENTS

Garlic cloves
Slices of rustic white bread,
    best toasted on a hot barbecue
Ripe tomatoes, halved
High-quality cold-pressed olive oil
Coarse salt

PREPARATION

If you like, halve a garlic clove and rub the toasted bread with the garlic. Then rub each slice of bread with the fruit of half a tomato. Discard the tomato skin – it isn't used in this recipe. Drizzle the bread generously with olive oil and sprinkle with a pinch of coarse salt – done.

Pan amb tomaquet makes an incredibly delicious and easy starter or snack.

MANDONGUILLES AMB PÉSOLS
ALBÓNDIGAS CON GUISANTES
MEATBALLS WITH PEAS

Who doesn't know and love delicious meatballs, served in a rich sauce?
The irresistible smell of these little delicacies wafts through many tapas bars in Barcelona.

Serves 4 | **Preparation:** 15 minutes | **Cooking and frying time:** 1 hour 5 minutes

INGREDIENTS
For the sauce

4 tablespoons olive oil

1 small red capsicum (pepper),
    finely diced

1 small green capsicum (pepper),
    finely diced

1 carrot, finely diced

2 tomatoes, finely diced

1 large onion, finely diced

1 small garlic clove, minced

200 ml (7 fl oz) vegetable stock

240 g (8½ oz) can peas

For the meatballs

1 egg

2 slices stale white bread, diced

½ glass white wine

1 kg (2 lb 4 oz) mixed minced
    (ground) meat

2 tablespoons plain (all-purpose)
    flour

PREPARE THE SAUCE

Heat 1 tablespoon olive oil in a saucepan over medium heat. Add the capsicums, carrot, tomatoes, onion and garlic and sauté for 6–8 minutes. Season with salt and freshly ground black pepper. Blend thoroughly with a stick blender and return to the saucepan. Add the vegetable stock and heat everything through.

PREPARE AND FRY THE MEATBALLS

Meanwhile, combine the egg, bread, white wine and a little salt in a bowl. Add the minced meat and knead everything to form a dough. Transfer the flour to a shallow plate. Shape the meat mixture into balls of about 4 cm (1½ inches) diameter. Roll in the flour to prevent them from falling apart during frying.

Heat the remaining olive oil in a deep frying pan over medium heat and fry the meatballs until golden brown. Transfer the meatballs to the sauce. Increase the heat slightly and cook the meatballs until done, about 30 minutes. Add the peas to the sauce and simmer for another 10 minutes. Serve hot in individual ceramic bowls.

VARIATION:

To make mandonguilles a la jardinera, only add half of the peas to the blended sauce before heating. Substitute the other half with diced carrot and add 150 g (5½ oz) small button mushrooms.

SEITONS EN VINAGRE
BOQUERONES EN VINAGRE
PICKLED ANCHOVIES

Seitons *or* boquerones en vinagre *are among the stand-out tapas in Barcelonian bars. The origins of this recipe, which was imported by migrant workers, can be traced back to Andalusia. Pickled in vinegar, oil, garlic and parsley and served on a slice of baguette rubbed with half a tomato, these anchovies are simply exquisite. They have been known to entice even people averse to fish, especially raw fish!*

Serves 4 | **Preparation:** 45 minutes | **Marinating time:** at least 4 hours

INGREDIENTS

500 g (1 lb 2 oz) fresh anchovies
    (ideally gutted by a fishmonger)
400 ml (14 fl oz) wine vinegar
1 teaspoon salt
1 garlic clove, thinly sliced
1 teaspoon sweet paprika
Cold-pressed olive oil
Flat-leaf (Italian) parsley, thinly
    sliced

PREPARE THE ANCHOVIES

Carefully wash the fresh anchovies and snap off the heads towards the spines. Use your thumb to slice open the fish from this opening towards the tail and remove the guts. Rinse the remaining fillets and remove the central bone and all attached bones, starting from the tail. It is easier, though, to have your fishmonger prepare the fish. Transfer the prepared anchovy fillets to a bowl with iced water and leave for about 20 minutes to remove any impurities.

MARINATE THE ANCHOVIES

Combine the wine vinegar, salt and garlic well in a ceramic or plastic bowl. Add the anchovies, refrigerate and marinate for at least 4 hours, but no more than 24 hours – if marinating for an extended period, dilute the marinade with a little more vinegar. The fish should be completely covered with the marinade.

PUT THE DISH TOGETHER

To serve, remove the anchovies from the marinade, but do not drain them. Reserve the marinade. Arrange the anchovies on a plate and dust with a little paprika to taste. Drizzle with olive oil and sprinkle with parsley and the sliced garlic from the marinade. As an alternative, serve on a slice of bread rubbed with half a tomato.

Covered with marinade or oil, these anchovies will keep for 2–3 days in the refrigerator.

GAMBAS AL AJILLO
GAMBAS AL AJILLO
PRAWNS IN GARLIC SAUCE

Gambas al ajillo *are not only among the best-known tapas,*
they are also easy to prepare and incredibly delicious.

Serves 4 | **Preparation:** 10 minutes | **Cooking time:** 15 minutes

INGREDIENTS

3 garlic cloves, thinly sliced

2 red chillies, seeded and
    thinly sliced

250 ml (9 fl oz) olive oil

100 g (3½ oz) prawns (shrimp),
    peeled and deveined with
    tails intact

PREPARATION

Gently fry the sliced garlic and chillies in a little of the olive oil in a deep frying pan
or casserole dish. Add the prawns as soon as the garlic starts to colour and briefly fry
everything together. Add the remaining olive oil, heat everything over medium heat
and season with a little salt. Serve immediately with white bread, either straight from
the pan or in four warmed ceramic bowls.

ENSALADILLA RUSA

ENSALADILLA RUSA
RUSSIAN SALAD

*Ensaladilla rusa is yet another popular tapa in bars all over Barcelona.
It was originally a way of using up leftovers.*

Serves 4 | **Preparation:** 10 minutes | **Chilling time:** 2–3 hours

INGREDIENTS

200 g (7 oz) waxy potatoes, boiled
and diced

300 g (10½ oz) green beans, cooked
and cut into short lengths

300 g (10½ oz) peas, cooked
(alternatively use canned peas)

300 g (10½ oz) carrots, cooked and
finely diced

1 tomato, peeled, seeded and
finely diced

Home-made mayonnaise (see
recipe on page 260)

PREPARATION

Toss all of the vegetables in a bowl to combine. Fold in the mayonnaise. Season with
salt and freshly ground white pepper.

Refrigerate the salad for 2–3 hours before serving.

PATATES BRAVES
PATATAS BRAVAS
PATATAS BRAVAS

Patatas bravas *are eaten all over Spain. These 'wild potatoes' are served with* salsa brava, *a flavourful sauce that should never see ketchup, even though these days it is (unfortunately) often replaced by a milder mixture of ketchup and tomatoes. Actually mayonnaise isn't a traditional ingredient either, but I just love it. The best-tasting and most popular* bravas *in all of Barcelona are served at 'Casa Tomás' in Sarrià, where they are prepared with* all i oli *instead of mayonnaise.*

Serves 4 | **Preparation:** 30 minutes | **Cooking and frying time:** 30 minutes

INGREDIENTS
For the salsa brava
2 tablespoons olive oil

1 onion, finely diced

1 tablespoon sweet paprika

1 tablespoon hot paprika

2–3 tablespoons plain (all-purpose) flour

100 g (3½ oz) canned tomato purée

400 ml (14 fl oz) chicken stock

For the potatoes
Olive oil for deep-frying

2 large potatoes, cut into 2.5 cm (1 inch) thick strips

Plus
Home-made mayonnaise (see recipe on page 260)

PREPARE THE SALSA BRAVA
Warm the olive oil in a frying pan over medium heat. Add the onion and sweat until translucent. Stir in the paprika carefully, as paprika burns easily and then turns bitter. Stir in the flour, then add the puréed tomatoes and chicken stock. Simmer to reduce a little. Season with salt. Salsa brava will keep for a good week in the refrigerator.

FRY AND PLATE THE POTATOES
Heat the olive oil in a deep frying pan or casserole dish over very high heat. Add the potatoes and fry for 2 minutes. Reduce the temperature and continue to cook for another 5–6 minutes. Increase the temperature again for the final 2 minutes until the potatoes turn golden brown.

Drain the potatoes on paper towel and season with salt. Serve with a dollop of mayonnaise and a generous drizzle of salsa brava.

BOMBETAS DE PATATES FARCIDAS
BOMBAS DE PATATAS RELLENAS
STUFFED POTATO BALLS

This delectably simple dish is a staple in many tapas bars. The potato balls can be served warm or cold. They are especially popular in the old town of Barcelona and in Barceloneta.

Makes 12–14 potato balls | **Preparation:** 25 minutes | **Cooking and frying time:** 30 minutes

INGREDIENTS

400 g (14 oz) floury potatoes

1 onion

1 small garlic clove

200 g (7 oz) mixed minced (ground)
    meat

100 g (3½ oz) canned tomato purée

1 teaspoon Tabasco sauce

Freshly ground nutmeg

Olive oil for frying and for the
    potato dough

3–4 tablespoons plain (all-purpose)
    flour

3–4 tablespoons breadcrumbs

2 eggs

Home-made mayonnaise (see
    recipe on page 260)

Salsa brava (see recipe on page 30)

PREPARE THE MINCED MEAT MIXTURE

Scrub the potatoes and boil until tender with the skins on. Meanwhile, peel and mince the onion and garlic. Heat a frying pan over medium heat. Add the onion, garlic and minced meat and fry briefly. Once the meat has browned all over, add the tomato purée and Tabasco and season with salt. Continue to cook for another 10 minutes, stirring constantly, until all of the liquid has evaporated.

MAKE AND COOK THE POTATO BALLS

Peel the cooked potatoes once they are cool enough to handle. Transfer to a bowl and mash thoroughly with a fork. Season well with salt, freshly ground black pepper, nutmeg and 1–2 tablespoons olive oil. This should make a soft dough that is still easy to shape.

Shape the potato dough into 12–14 balls. Flatten the balls and place a small amount of the minced meat mixture in the centre. Carefully shape into balls again around the filling. Transfer the flour and breadcrumbs to separate shallow bowls. Whisk the eggs in a third bowl. Turn the balls in the flour, then dip them into the whisked eggs and roll them in the breadcrumbs.

Deep-fry the balls in plenty of olive oil over high heat until golden brown. Drain on paper towel. Serve with home-made mayonnaise and salsa brava.

PIMIENTOS DE PADRÓN
PIMIENTOS DE PADRÓN
DEEP-FRIED PADRÓN CHILLIES

Pimientos de padrón originally come from the region around the city of Padrón. Until about 20 years ago, they were mainly found in Galician tapas bars in Barcelona, but these days they are a fixture on the menu of virtually any tapas bar in the city. Part of the original fun was that padrón chillies used to be rather unpredictable. About one in six or eight chillies on the plate would be hot, and about one in ten or twelve fiercely so — but there was no way of telling from just looking. Any hot surprises were taken in good spirits, though, and with a lot of laughter. These days, pimientos de padrón are available from many well-stocked greengrocers and supermarkets.

Serves 4 | **Preparation:** 15 minutes | **Deep-frying time:** 5 minutes

INGREDIENTS
250 g (9 oz) padrón chillies

Olive oil for deep-frying

Fleur de sel

PREPARATION
Wash the chillies and dry well. Heat the olive oil in a saucepan or deep-fryer and fry the chillies until the skins begin to blister all over and develop a few dark brown spots. Briefly drain on paper towel. Transfer to a plate, sprinkle with coarse fleur de sel salt and serve immediately.

PEOPLE

love to

ARE AL

BEST

WHO

eat

ays THE

PEOPLE

OUS ESTRELLATS
HUEVOS ESTRELLADOS
FRIED EGGS AND POTATOES

Eggs and potatoes always make an excellent combination for which there seems to exist an endless variety of recipes. The 'Vermutería Lou' won a prize for this recipe in the 2014 Barcelona tapas competition. Try it and you'll know why!

Serves 4 | **Preparation:** 10 minutes | **Cooking time:** 15 minutes

INGREDIENTS

Plenty of olive oil

4 potatoes, cut into 2.5 cm (1 inch) dice or into chips

4 very fresh eggs

Iberian ham, cut into thin strips

FRY THE POTATOTES

Heat plenty of olive oil in a deep frying pan or casserole dish over very high heat. Add the potatoes and fry for 2 minutes over high heat. Reduce the temperature and cook the potatoes for another 5–6 minutes. Increase the temperature again and cook for another 2 minutes until the potatoes are golden brown. Drain the potatoes on paper towel and season with salt.

FRY THE EGGS

Heat plenty of olive oil in another frying pan. Crack the eggs and slide into the pan. Fry, continually basting with hot olive oil. The idea is to have the egg whites set fully while keeping the egg yolks beautifully runny.

Divide the potatoes among four ceramic bowls. Slide 1 egg on top of each. Season the eggs with a little salt and top with strips of ham. Serve immediately. Allow the hot egg yolks to burst over the potatoes, if preferred.

BRANDADA DE BACALAO

BRANDADA DE BACALAO
PURÉED BACALAO

There are a number of different versions of brandada de bacalao, *all of which make popular starters across the region extending from the Basque country to Catalonia and Catalan-speaking France. This easy recipe is always a winner.*

Serves 4 | **Preparation:** 20 minutes | **Cooking time:** 25 minutes

INGREDIENTS

400 g (14 oz) bacalao (salt cod),
   desalted, without skin or bones,
   diced
250 g (9 oz) floury potatoes
300 ml (10½ fl oz) olive oil
1 garlic clove, thinly sliced
100 ml (3½ fl oz) cream, gently
   warmed

COOK THE BACALAO

Bring plenty of water to the boil in a pot. Add the bacalao and simmer for 2 minutes, making sure that it is well covered with water. Remove the bacalao and drain well. Reserve a little of the cooking water.

BOIL THE POTATOES

Peel the potatoes and boil them in a pan of salted water. Meanwhile, heat the olive oil in a saucepan over medium heat. Gently fry the garlic slices until golden brown, being careful not to burn them, as they then turn bitter. Remove from the oil and set aside.

Remove the saucepan from the heat and add the bacalao to the hot oil. The fish will cook perfectly in the heat retained in the oil.

Drain the potatoes. Combine with the cream and mash thoroughly. If necessary or preferred, add a little of the reserved cooking liquid. Season to taste with salt and freshly ground white pepper.

PUT TOGETHER THE BRANDADA

Transfer the mashed potatoes, bacalao and garlic to a blender. Blend well. Add the olive oil to the running blender in a steady stream until the cream firms up a little. Season to taste with salt and white pepper.

Spread thickly on slices of toasted baguette and garnish with parsley, pickled capsicums or caviar. Alternatively, serve with sliced potatoes and paprika.

PIMIENTOS DEL PIQUILLO FARCITS
PIMIENTOS DEL PIQUILLO RELLENOS
STUFFED PIQUILLO PEPPERS

*In Barcelona, there is no tapas bar worth its salt that does not feature this little delicacy on its menu.
Pimientos del piquillo are made of red piquillo peppers, which are about 7–10 cm (2¾–4 inches) long
and whose shape is reminiscent of liberty caps. Raw piquillos are too bitter for eating, so they are first
roasted over an open fire and then peeled and seeded by hand. This gives them a mild, smoky aroma and
a pleasantly spicy, sweet and sour flavour. Piquillos are only available in jars or cans. They can be stuffed
with a variety of fillings and used for any number of wonderful tapas and starters.*

Serves 2 | **Preparation:** 1½ hours | **Cooking time:** 15 minutes

INGREDIENTS
For the pimientos
100 ml (3½ fl oz) olive oil, plus
    extra for sautéing and frying
300 g (10½ oz) bacalao (salt cod),
    desalted, without skin or
    bones, cut into two pieces
150 ml (5 fl oz) cream
2–3 garlic cloves, peeled
1 dried chilli
2 tablespoons flat-leaf (Italian)
    parsley, finely chopped
8 red piquillo peppers

For the sauce
100 ml (3½ fl oz) olive oil
2 garlic cloves, thinly sliced
2 red piquillo peppers
300 ml (10½ fl oz) cream

COOK THE BACALAO
Heat the olive oil in a frying pan over low heat, making sure the temperature never exceeds 90°C (195°F). Add the bacalao to the oil. (Alternatively, remove the pan from the heat and gently cook the bacalao in the residual heat, gently shaking the pan.) The fish will release a milky liquid, which will emulsify with the oil. Carefully turn the fish after 10 minutes, then continue cooking for another 5 minutes. Remove the fish from the oil and set aside to cool.

Meanwhile, heat the cream in a saucepan over low heat and reduce carefully. Heat a little olive oil in another pan over very low heat. Add the garlic and chilli and sauté until golden to flavour the oil. Discard the garlic and chilli.

PREPARE THE FILLING
Carefully pull the bacalao into pieces with a fork, removing and discarding the skin. Transfer to a bowl and combine with the chopped parsley. Slowly add the flavoured oil and the reduced cream and whisk everything to combine to a thick paste. Season with salt and freshly ground white pepper. Use a piping bag or small spoon to fill the piquillo peppers about three-quarters full with the bacalao mixture. Set aside.

Preheat the oven to 160°C (320°F).

PREPARE THE SAUCE

For the sauce, heat the olive oil in a saucepan over medium heat. Add the garlic and gently fry until golden brown. Remove from the oil. Add the piquillo peppers to the hot oil. Add the cream and simmer for 5 minutes, then season with salt and white pepper. Blend everything well with a stick blender, then reduce a little more.

Arrange the stuffed peppers in a ceramic bowl, spoon the sauce on top and place in the hot oven to heat through for a few minutes before serving.

ESQUEIXADA
ESQUEIXADA
BACALAO AND VEGETABLE SALAD

An esqueixada, *pronounced 'es-cay-shah-da', is a unique type of salad. It is prepared with desalted, raw bacalao and various vegetables. Not only does it take next to no time to prepare, it also makes a very refreshing and healthy snack on a hot summer's day. Like many other simple, classic dishes, esqueixada also comes in many different versions, so feel free to experiment with any seasonal vegetables you like.*

Serves 4 | **Preparation:** 15 minutes | **Marinating time:** 30 minutes

INGREDIENTS

300 g (10½ oz) tomatoes

600 g (1 lb 5 oz) bacalao (salt cod),
    desalted, without skin or bones

1 green capsicum (pepper)

1 red capsicum (pepper)

2 red onions

200 ml (7 fl oz) olive oil

4 tablespoons vinegar

150 g (5½ oz) black olives, diced

PREPARATION

Dice the tomatoes finely. Squeeze out the excess water from the bacalao and cut it into bite-sized pieces. Refrigerate the diced tomatoes and fish.

Trim the capsicums and onions and finely dice. Transfer to a bowl, dress with olive oil and vinegar and toss to combine. Season with salt and freshly ground black pepper.

Refrigerate for 30 minutes to allow the flavours to marry, then put the dish together using ring moulds. First add the tomatoes to the moulds, followed by the bacalao. Top with the marinated vegetables and press down gently. Drizzle with the marinade and garnish with the olives. Remove the ring moulds before serving.

XIPS DE CARXOFES
CHIPS DE ALCACHOFAS
ARTICHOKE CHIPS

Barcelona is truly blessed with its location, with the Mediterranean Sea on one side and the Baix-Llobregat, the fertile delta of the Llobregat river, in the city's south-west. Farmers have produced excellent vegetables in this delta for centuries. Particularly good are the local habas *(broad beans) and artichokes, which even have their own denomination of origin (DO). In good years with mild winters, fresh artichokes are available as early as December — and as cheap as potatoes! Artichokes deserve a lot better than being drowned in a vinaigrette. Deep-fried artichokes, for example, are a lot healthier than potato chips and a lot tastier, too. A thoroughly delectable tapa!*

Serves 4 | **Preparation:** 10 minutes | **Deep-frying time:** 5 minutes

INGREDIENTS
4–8 small Spanish artichokes
Olive oil or sunflower oil for
    deep-frying

PREPARATION
Clean and trim the artichokes. Remove the fibrous chokes and cut the hearts lengthwise into 3 mm (⅛ inch) slices. Heat the oil in a saucepan and quickly add the sliced artichokes to prevent oxidation. Deep-fry until golden brown. Drain on paper towel, season with a little salt and serve hot.

I always suggest that people wear gloves when working with artichokes. Spotty brown hands aren't a great sight.

CAPDELLS AMB CABRALES AL FORN

COGOLLOS CON CABRALES AL HORNO
BAKED LETTUCE HEARTS WITH CABRALES

Cabrales, an intensely flavoured blue-vein cheese, comes from the village of the same name. When still young, it tastes like a mild gorgonzola. As it matures, it develops a fuller flavour, similar to roquefort, and fully mature it becomes quite strong. Witlof (chicory) makes an excellent alternative for preparing this dish.

Serves 4 | **Preparation:** 15 minutes | **Cooking time:** 5 minutes

INGREDIENTS

4 small cos (romaine) lettuce hearts
Cabrales or other blue-vein cheese
    to taste

PREPARATION

Preheat the oven grill (broiler) to medium heat.

Remove any tough or unsightly outer leaves from the lettuce hearts. Wash and shake dry the lettuces. Halve or quarter, depending on size, and top with cheese to taste. Cook under the preheated grill for a few minutes and serve immediately.

PA ROSTIT AMB PATE DE TOMAQUET
PAN TOSTADO CON PATÉ DE TOMATE
GRILLED BREAD WITH TOMATO PASTE

Barcelona is a very creative city in every respect, and so it doesn't come as a surprise that cafés and bars also display almost unlimited ingenuity when it comes to tapas. One of these cafés is 'Caelum, delicias y otras tentaciones de Monasterio', and its name says it all: 'heaven, delicacies and other temptations from the monastery'. This is also precisely its mission, as the café offers beverages, sweets, pastries and more, all made in local monasteries, for enjoying on the premises or taking home. Its kitchen is the home of this elegant starter: toasted bread with tomato paste and brie.

Serves 4 | **Preparation:** 15 minutes | **Cooking time:** 5 minutes

INGREDIENTS

4 sun-dried tomatoes in oil, drained
1 anchovy fillet in oil
Mushroom powder to taste
100 g (3½ oz) black olive paste
1 baguette, sliced diagonally into
   8 pieces
200 g (7 oz) brie cheese

PREPARATION

Slice the tomatoes and anchovy fillet as thinly as possible. Pound both to a paste using a mortar and pestle. Season with mushroom powder to taste. Add the olive paste and mix to combine.

Preheat the oven grill (broiler) to medium heat. Cut the brie into slices to fit the baguette slices. Top each baguette slice with a slice of brie. Spread generously with the tomato and olive paste. Cook under the preheated grill until the cheese starts to melt. Serve immediately.

ANEM DE TAPES...

... is what people say in Barcelona when they want to catch up with friends, have a drink and eat a couple of tapas. What then usually happens is that they move from one bar to the next, and a glass of wine or just one beer with a few tapas quickly turns into a full dinner and a cheerful evening in great company.

One of Barcelona's most beautiful quarters, El Born/ La Ribera, is home to quite a few very typical tapas bars. There is 'El Xampanyet' opposite the Picasso museum, a true classic, or the 'Sagardí', which serves Basque tapas on thick slices of white bread. Everyone helps themselves, and at the end the bill is prepared by counting the empty *palillos* (skewers).

PAQUETS DE FABES
PAQUETES DE HABAS
BROAD BEAN PARCELS

Barcelona wouldn't be Barcelona if it wasn't constantly reinventing itself. While this version of habas a la catalana *is admittedly simple, it can still take its pride of place next to fancier tapas. It makes an innovative starter or snack and will definitely surprise your guests.*

Serves 4 | **Preparation:** 10 minutes | **Cooking time:** 40 minutes

INGREDIENTS

Meat stock

350 g (12 oz) small broad beans, shelled

9 large slices of jamón Canario or shoulder of ham, plus extra if very thin

6–8 fresh mint leaves

Olive oil for frying

PREPARATION

Heat the meat stock in a saucepan, add the broad beans and cook for 20–30 minutes over medium heat until soft. Drain well. Season with a little salt, if necessary.

Cut one slice of ham into small pieces and coarsely chop a few of the mint leaves. Combine the chopped ham and mint leaves with the cooked beans.

Divide the bean mixture among eight slices of ham. Make small parcels out of the slices by first folding in the sides on top of the beans, and then folding the ends on top. If the ham is sliced very thinly and tears, place the parcel on top of another slice of ham, seam side down, and repeat the process.

Heat a frying pan over medium heat. Add the olive oil and fry the parcels, seam side down, until crisp. Turn and fry the other side until crisp. Garnish with the remaining mint and serve, if desired, on a bed of the cooked beans.

PATATA, TOMAQUET I SEITONS
PATATAS, TOMATE Y BOQUERONES
POTATO STACKS WITH ANCHOVIES AND TOMATOES

Many tapas, including these boquerones, *can be easily turned into delicious starters.*
The version described in this recipe makes a simple yet perfect summer dish.

Serves 4 | **Preparation:** 15 minutes

INGREDIENTS

Baby English spinach for garnish

4 potatoes, boiled, peeled and cut
  into 1 cm (½ inch) slices (the
  ends are not used in this recipe)

8 sun-dried tomatoes in oil, drained

8 whole anchovies in vinegar (do not
  substitute with salted anchovies)

A little finely diced Iberian ham
  for garnish

Sea salt flakes

Coarsely ground pink pepper

Olive oil

Vinegar

PREPARATION

Lay out the baby spinach in overlapping circles on four plates. Arrange the potato slices, sun-dried tomatoes and anchovies on top of the spinach in alternating layers. This should eventually look similar to the picture on the right. Use a toothpick or skewer to hold the stacks together, if necessary.

Sprinkle the spinach and the potato stacks with some diced ham, sea salt flakes and pink pepper.

Prepare a vinaigrette from olive oil, vinegar, pepper and salt and drizzle over the spinach to make a refreshing summer starter.

FLAN DE GAROÏNES

FLAN DE ERIZOS DE MAR
SEA URCHIN FLAN

An encounter with a sea urchin generally makes for holiday memories that most would rather forget. But there's another way! In spring, people along the Costa Brava organise garoïnades or sea urchin dinners, where each family and each town showcases the best recipes. Sea urchins are true delicacies that do not come cheap, and all that is used for cooking is the sea urchin ovaries, that is the gonads or roe, and the liquid inside. Sea urchins taste neither of fish nor of mussels or caviar, but simply and incomparably of the sea.

Serves 4 | **Preparation:** 15 minutes | **Cooking and baking time:** 45 minutes

INGREDIENTS

For the flan

12 fresh sea urchins

500 ml (17 fl oz) cream

2 g (1⁄16 oz) saffron

2 eggs

3 egg yolks

Oil or butter for the moulds

For the side

Salad leaves

Vinegar

Olive oil

EXTRACT THE SEA URCHIN ROE

Use a cloth or tea towel to grab the sea urchin with your left hand. Hold it so that the flat bottom is pointing upwards.

Use scissors to cut a circle around the mouth. Pull out this disc together with the attached innards and discard.

Strain the liquid inside the sea urchin through a sieve and reserve.

Inside the sea urchin you'll see five pale orange or red tongue-shaped sections. These are its roe. Carefully remove these using a small spoon. Set aside.

PREPARE THE FLAN

Preheat the oven to 180°C (350°F). Combine the cream and saffron in a saucepan and bring to the boil. Transfer the eggs, egg yolks and sea urchin roe to a bowl and blend with a stick blender. Whisk in the warm saffron cream, then season with salt and freshly ground white pepper.

Divide the mixture among four greased ramekins and bake in the preheated oven for 40 minutes or until set. The cooking time will depend on the size and material of the ramekins – keep checking whether the flans are done by inserting a sharp knife. Remove from the oven, leave to cool and serve with some salad leaves drizzled with a simple vinaigrette of vinegar, olive oil, salt and freshly ground black pepper.

BROMERA DE GAROÏNES
ESPUMA DE ERIZOS DE MAR
SEA URCHIN FOAM

Sea urchin foam is probably the most exquisite of all tapas. It is decoratively served inside the sea urchin shells on a bed of salt. Carefully and evenly enlarge the openings of the sea urchins with sharp kitchen scissors to use the shells for serving.

Serves 4 | **Preparation:** 20 minutes

INGREDIENTS

16 fresh sea urchins
2 egg yolks
4 tablespoons pink cava or
    sparkling rosé wine
4 tablespoons cream
Salt to serve

PREPARATION

Remove the sea urchin roe as described on page 58. Clean four of the sea urchin shells and set aside.

Whisk the egg yolks and cava in a double boiler until foamy. Continue whisking until the mixture has the consistency of a sabayon.

Beat the sea urchin roe and cream until foamy using an electric mixer. Pour into a saucepan and heat over low heat, then combine with the 'sabayon'.

Pour the warm mixture into the cleaned shells and serve on a bed of salt, with a teaspoon for eating.

CREMA DE GAROÏNAS
CREMA DE ERIZOS DE MAR
SEA URCHIN CREAM SOUP

*Sea urchin can be prepared in a surprising variety of ways. Try this as
a soup or use the recipe to make a rather extravagant sauce for fish.*

Serves 4 | **Preparation:** 20 minutes | **Cooking time:** 15 minutes

INGREDIENTS

8 fresh sea urchins

10 g (¼ oz) butter

1 French shallot, finely diced

150 ml (5 fl oz) dry white wine

650 ml (22½ fl oz) fish stock
   (see recipe on page 261)

2 tablespoons crème fraîche

2 egg yolks

PREPARATION

Remove the sea urchin roe as described on page 58, reserving the strained liquid.

Heat a casserole dish over medium heat. Melt the butter, add the diced shallot and sauté briefly. Deglaze with the wine and reduce by half. Add the fish stock and sea urchin liquid and reduce a little.

Whisk the crème fraîche with the egg yolks until smooth, then gradually whisk the mixture into the stock mixture. Do not allow the mixture to return to the boil, otherwise the egg yolk may curdle.

Strain the thickened soup through a sieve and beat with a stick blender until light and airy. Season with salt and freshly ground white pepper to taste. Just before serving, stir in the sea urchin roe.

If you reduce the amount of fish stock to about 250 ml (9 fl oz) and leave the mixture to reduce a little more, you will have a delicate, creamy sauce with an intense aroma of sea urchin. This sauce matches perfectly with poached or steamed sole or turbot. You'll only need to use four sea urchins.

CREMA DE CARXOFES
CREMA DE ALCACHOFAS
ARTICHOKE CREAM SOUP

Artichokes are a wonderful vegetable. If it pains you to waste the trimmed petals, this soup is an excellent solution.

Serves 4 | **Preparation:** 25 minutes | **Cooking time:** 55 minutes

INGREDIENTS

4 artichokes

Juice of ½ lemon

½ garlic clove, crushed

1 pinch salt

2 tablespoons olive oil

25 g (1 oz) butter

2 onions, chopped

400 ml (14 fl oz) chicken or
   vegetable stock

1 pinch cayenne pepper

20 g (¾ oz) plain (all-purpose) flour

250 ml (9 fl oz) cream

2 tablespoons flat-leaf (Italian)
   parsley

PREPARE THE ARTICHOKES

Cut off and peel the artichoke stems and immediately drop them into a bowl of water with half of the lemon juice added. Remove the artichoke petals and peel them down to the hearts. Also remove the inner petals directly above the artichoke hearts. Immediately drop the petals into the bowl of acidulated water to prevent them from oxidising. Remove and discard the fibrous chokes from the hearts.

Combine 1 litre (35 fl oz) water, the remaining lemon juice, garlic, salt and olive oil in a large saucepan and bring to the boil. Add the artichoke hearts and stems. Simmer for about 25 minutes or until they can be easily pierced with a fork, but still hold their shape. Remove from the saucepan and set aside. Add the artichoke petals to the saucepan, bring to the boil and simmer for 25 minutes over low heat. Remove the petals from the cooking liquid and blend them to a fine paste using a stick blender. Pass the paste through a sieve. Strain the cooking liquid through a sieve and reserve 350 ml (12 fl oz). Slice the artichoke hearts and dice the stems. Set aside.

FINISH THE ARTICHOKE CREAM SOUP

Melt the butter in a saucepan over medium heat. Add the onions and sauté briefly. Add the stock, artichoke paste and reserved cooking liquid and season with salt and cayenne pepper. Combine the flour with a little cream and whisk into the soup to thicken. Add the remaining cream and briefly bring to the boil, adding the sliced artichoke hearts and diced stems just before the mixture comes to the boil. Serve garnished with parsley.

CREMA DE CARXOFES I CURRI
CREMA DE ALCACHOFAS Y CURRY
CURRIED ARTICHOKE CREAM

Artichokes are an incredibly versatile vegetable that can be combined with many different ingredients and spices – in this case with curry.

Serves 4 | **Preparation:** 20 minutes | **Cooking time:** 1 hour 10 minutes

INGREDIENTS

4 artichokes

Juice of 1 lemon

2 tablespoons olive oil

1 onion, finely diced

200 g (7 oz) carrots, diced

2 tablespoons curry powder,
   plus a little extra for garnish

400 g (14 oz) potatoes, diced

500 ml (17 fl oz) vegetable stock

250 ml (9 fl oz) cream

2 tablespoons flat-leaf (Italian)
   parsley

PREPARE AND COOK THE ARTICHOKES

Cut off and peel the artichoke stems and immediately drop them into a bowl of water with half of the lemon juice added. Remove the artichoke petals and peel them down to the hearts. Also remove the inner petals directly above the artichoke hearts. Immediately drop the petals into the bowl of acidulated water to prevent them from oxidising. Remove and discard the fibrous chokes from the hearts.

Cook the artichoke hearts and stems in boiling salted water for 10–12 minutes. Remove from the saucepan and refresh under cold water. Add the petals to the saucepan and cook until soft, about 25 minutes. Remove the petals from the cooking liquid and blend them to a paste using a stick blender. Pass the paste through a sieve. Strain the cooking liquid through a sieve and reserve 400 ml (14 fl oz).

FINISH THE ARTICHOKE CREAM

Heat the olive oil in a saucepan over medium heat. Add the onion and carrots and sauté briefly. Stir in the curry powder and add the potatoes. Add the vegetable stock, artichoke paste and reserved artichoke cooking liquid. Reduce the heat and simmer the mixture for about 20 minutes. Add the artichoke stems and blend the mixture. Stir the cream into the soup. Slice the artichoke hearts lengthwise and heat them in the soup. Season with salt and a little freshly ground black pepper and serve garnished with parsley and curry powder.

TAPAS BARS

Tapas, or little 'lids' (which is what the words translates as) made of cured meat, ham or bread that were once placed on top of wine glasses to keep bothersome flies out, have developed an amazing life of their own over time. And there is no end in sight to their success story. An entirely new type of restaurant has developed that specialises only in *tapas*. After all, *tapas* is something you can have at any time, as a sit-down meal, on the go or standing at a bar, which is the preferred way by far. Once you start nibbling on these little morsels as an appetiser before your actual dinner, it's all too easy to forget about having a proper meal altogether, as tapas bars are synonymous with a lively, fun-filled atmosphere that makes it difficult to leave.

TAPAS
€1
Mediterranean cuisine
Petites Bitels · Petits Verns

Bastaix   BAR DE VINS, TAPES I COPES

TARTAR
DEL DIA

VINS
APEROLS
I COPES

Peix de
mercat

TAPAS

CREMA DE MONGETES
CREMA DE ALUBIAS
CREAMED CANNELLINI BEANS

*Legumes have always played an important role in Spanish cuisine and, luckily for us,
they have never been quite relegated from this role. This recipe uses canned white beans.
If you prefer to use dried beans, make sure you soak them overnight first. I like using a
flavourful chicken stock, but this tasty dish can also be prepared with vegetarian stock.
These creamed beans can be served as a starter or main course.*

Serves 8 | **Preparation:** 10 minutes | **Cooking time:** 20 minutes

INGREDIENTS

2 x 400 g (14 oz) cans cannellini
   beans
100 ml (3½ fl oz) strong chicken
   stock (or vegetable stock)
100 ml (3½ fl oz) dry white wine
1 small sprig thyme
1–2 tablespoons walnut oil
4 small slices serrano ham,
   oven-dried

PREPARATION

Add the beans and their liquid to a small casserole dish. Add a little of the stock and
white wine and the sprig of thyme. Cook for 15 minutes over high heat, but be careful
not to burn the mixture. Mash the beans with a potato masher.

Remove the thyme and pass the beans through a sieve. Discard any skins remaining
in the sieve. Season the resulting cream with more stock and wine, but be careful not to
let it get too runny. Add enough walnut oil to give the mixture a creamy consistency.
Transfer the mixture to a saucepan and warm over low heat. Serve garnished with pieces
of dried ham.

VARIATION

If you make the cream a little thinner and lighter by adding more stock or wine, this
makes a flavoursome soup that will serve 4. Alternatively, add more oil to taste to make
it a little richer.

SOPA FREDDA AMB ALFABERGA
SOPA FRÍA CON ALBAHACA
CHILLED HERB SOUP

I was once served this chilled Catalan vegetarian soup made according to a recipe by Carme Ruscalleda, one of Barcelona's best-known chefs. It makes a delicious tapa on hot summer days. The ground pine nuts and oil give it a deliciously creamy consistency.

Serves 4–6 | **Preparation:** 25 minutes | **Cooking time:** 30 minutes | **Chilling time:** 1–2 hours

INGREDIENTS
For the vegetable stock

150 g (5½ oz) carrots
150 g (5½ oz) leek
150 g (5½ oz) onions
Olive oil for frying
A few sprigs of parsley,
    finely chopped
1 garlic clove, peeled
2 litres (70 fl oz) boiling water

For the herb mixture

100 g (3½ oz) pine nuts
220 ml (7½ fl oz) olive oil
¼ garlic clove
40 g (1½ oz) flat-leaf (Italian)
    parsley, leaves picked and
    chopped
40 g (1½ oz) basil leaves, chopped
10 g (¼ oz) salt

PREPARE THE VEGETABLE STOCK

Trim, peel and dice the vegetables. Heat the olive oil in a large saucepan over high heat. Add the vegetables, parsley and garlic clove and sear for 3 minutes. Add the boiling water and simmer everything for about 30 minutes. Season with a little salt and strain through a sieve. Set aside to cool and then refrigerate.

PREPARE THE HERB MIXTURE

Finely grind the pine nuts in a blender, then gradually add the olive oil, blending continuously. Add the garlic and herbs and blend in with some of the strained stock. Add the remaining stock and season with salt and freshly ground white pepper. Mix thoroughly. Serve chilled, but not ice cold.

PATATAS AL POBRE
PATATAS AL POBRE
POOR MAN'S POTATOES

Poor man's potatoes are a tasty, rich accompaniment to a wide variety of fish
and meat dishes. And often they're delicious enough just by themselves.

Serves 4 | **Cooking time:** 20–25 minutes

INGREDIENTS

200 g (7 oz) onions

400 g (14 oz) waxy potatoes

Olive oil for frying

1 red capsicum (pepper), cut into
    strips

1 green capsicum (pepper), cut into
    strips

1–2 garlic cloves, crushed

2 tablespoons vinegar

PREPARATION

Peel and roughly chop the onions. Wash the potatoes thoroughly and slice.

Warm the olive oil in a casserole dish over medium heat. Add the onion pieces and sweat until translucent. Add the potatoes and season with salt. Cook for 12–15 minutes. Add the capsicum strips and garlic, to taste. Continue to cook for another 5–10 minutes. Carefully shake the dish occasionally to prevent the vegetables from burning. Right at the end, add the vinegar and season to taste with more salt.

COCA

COCA
SAVOURY FLATBREADS

Coca is a type of flatbread that is popular all across Catalonia. It originated on the Balearic Isles and is quite similar to pizza. Coca is always made from a yeast dough, which is then topped with vegetables, fish or meat. There are innumerable varieties: square, round and oblong shapes with a thin and crispy or thicker and softer base, with sweet or savoury toppings. Often, coca toppings simply consist of left-over ingredients from the previous day, but there's one thing that NEVER goes on a coca, and that's cheese.

Serves 4 | **Preparation:** 10 minutes | **Marinating time:** 2 hours
Rising time: 40 minutes | **Baking time:** 25 minutes

INGREDIENTS
For the topping
Fresh or dried Mediterranean herbs
    (rosemary, bay leaf and, above
    all, thyme)
1 garlic clove, thinly sliced
100 ml (3½ fl oz) olive oil
Red capsicum (pepper), peeled or
    from a jar, cut into strips

For the dough
20 g (¾ oz) fresh yeast
1 pinch sugar
500 g (1 lb 2 oz) plain (all-purpose)
    flour
1 teaspoon salt
2 tablespoons olive oil
2 tablespoons white wine
Oil and flour for the benchtop
    and baking tray

PREPARE THE HERB OIL
Marinate the herbs and garlic in the olive oil for 1–2 hours. Remove the garlic, if preferred, or leave in the oil.

PREPARE THE YEAST DOUGH
Dissolve the yeast and sugar in 250 ml (9 fl oz) warm water in a small bowl. Add the flour and salt to a large mixing bowl and make a well in the centre. Pour the dissolved yeast into the well, combine with a little flour to make a starter and leave to rise for 10 minutes at room temperature. Add the olive oil and white wine and combine all ingredients. Knead to make a smooth dough. Cover and set aside to rise in a warm spot until the dough has doubled in volume. This will take about 30 minutes.

BAKE THE COCA
Preheat the oven to 180°C (350°F). Briefly knead the dough once more and roll it out thinly on a surface dusted with flour. Transfer to a baking tray and pierce all over with a fork. Leave to rise for another 10 minutes.

Spread the base generously with the herb oil and herbs. Divide the capsicum evenly over the base and bake the *coca* for 20–25 minutes.

Alternative, top the base with any tasty combination of blanched spinach, pine nuts and raisins, salt and pepper, or capsicum, onions and cured meats, sardines, tuna or smoked mackerel – there's no limit to your imagination.

OUS FREGITS AMB SAMFAINA

HUEVOS FRITOS CON SAMFAINA
FRIED EGGS ON SAMFAINA

*This dish is very easy to make and absolutely delicious, especially for breakfast
after a long night out. Basic restaurants often serve it as a starter, but I love it
for brunch and often dish it up in two different versions.*

Serves 4 | **Preparation:** 10 minutes

INGREDIENTS

Samfaina (see recipe on page 263)

4 eggs

Olive oil

Bread

VERSION 1

The day before, prepare the samfaina according to the recipe. Reheat in a saucepan.

Fry 1 egg per person in a frying pan with olive oil. Keep dousing the egg with the hot oil to ensure that the egg white sets and the egg yolk stays runny.

Lift the egg from the oil. Allow excess oil to drain. Season with salt and freshly ground black pepper and serve in a bowl on top of the samfaina. Serve with bread.

I LIKE VERSION 2 EVEN BETTER!

Reheat the samfaina in a ceramic casserole dish over medium heat. It shouldn't be too thick: thin with a splash of white wine, if necessary. Gently slide 1 very fresh egg per person into the boiling samfaina and poach. The eggs are ready once the egg whites have set and the yolks are still runny. Serve with a slice of toasted bread for breakfast.

TRUITA DE PATATES

TORTILLA DE PATATAS
POTATO TORTILLA

Tortillas are classics of Spanish cooking that are also very popular in Barcelona.
They only require very few ingredients, are easy to prepare and always taste delicious.

Serves 4 | **Preparation:** 10 minutes | **Resting time:** 1 hour | **Cooking time:** 40 minutes

INGREDIENTS

800 g (1 lb 12 oz) potatoes
2–3 onions
125 ml (4 fl oz) olive oil
6 eggs

PREPARATION

Peel the potatoes and onions. Cut the potatoes into small dice or thin slices and dice the onions finely.

Heat 4 tablespoons of the olive oil in a frying pan over medium heat. Add the potatoes and onions and cook for about 20–25 minutes. Do not allow them to brown.

Season the mixture with salt and freshly ground black pepper and transfer to a large bowl. Whisk the eggs and combine with the potatoes. Set aside to rest for about 1 hour.

Heat the remaining olive oil in the pan over medium heat. Add the potato mixture and cook until set, about 5–8 minutes. Turn the tortilla and cook the other side.

Tortillas can be eaten warm or cold. Slice into wedges or cut into tapas-sized cubes for serving.

TRUITA D'ESPÀRRECS
TORTILLA DE ESPARRAGOS
WILD ASPARAGUS TORTILLA

Once the days get noticeably longer again around the middle or end of January and there has been plenty of rain, people often come home from walks with large bunches of wild asparagus, which grows everywhere around Barcelona. It is a lot more aromatic and flavoursome than the cultivated green asparagus commonly available from shops. Wild asparagus is just fabulous in a tortilla. Unfortunately wild asparagus can be difficult to get in Australia, but standard green asparagus will do just fine.

Serves 4 | **Preparation:** 15 minutes | **Cooking time:** 10 minutes

INGREDIENTS

1 bunch wild asparagus (or thin green asparagus)

6 eggs

Olive oil

1 onion, finely diced

1 small garlic clove, crushed

PREPARATION

Wash the asparagus. Trim off the hard ends and slice the asparagus diagonally into short segments. Whisk the eggs together.

Heat the olive oil in a frying pan over high heat. Add the asparagus, onion and garlic and fry for about 5 minutes. Season with salt and drain on paper towel.

Transfer the fried vegetables to a bowl and combine with the eggs. Reheat the pan with a little oil over low heat. Return the mixture to the pan and cook until set. Flip over and cook the other side. This *truita d'espàrrecs* tastes great at any time of the day, warm or cold.

els millors
espàrrecs
d'en Roca

els millo
espàrr

TRUITA CATALANA AL ESTIL DE LA YAYA

TORTILLA A LA CATALANA DE LA ABUELA
GRANDMA'S TORTILLA

Grandma's truita catalana *is yet another version of tortilla, but quite a bit richer. It is not often found on restaurant menus, as it involves a little more work, but it's definitely worth it!*

Serves 4 | **Preparation:** 10 minutes | **Cooking time:** 25 minutes

INGREDIENTS

1 can white beans (mongetes/
   alubias), about 500 g (1 lb 2 oz)
1 piece of air-dried meat or smoked
   bacon, about 12 x 1 cm (4½ x
   ½ inch), cut into small pieces
1 piece raw sausage, preferably
   butifarra, about 10 cm (4 inches)
   long, cut into 5–7 pieces
5 very fresh eggs
2 tablespoons olive oil, plus extra
   for drizzling
Tomatoes to taste as a side dish

PREPARATION

Drain the beans through a sieve. Heat a frying pan over high heat. Add the drained beans, dried meat and sausage and sweat briefly. Whisk the eggs in a bowl, then stir in the beans and meat, together with a little salt. Stir carefully to combine.

Heat the olive oil in a frying pan. Add the egg mixture and and move it around carefully with a wooden spoon until set. As soon as the tortilla is golden-brown on one side, flip it over using a plate and cook it on the other side.

Serve the tortilla lukewarm, together with sliced or quartered tomatoes and a little best-quality olive oil, preferably made from arbequina olives.

XATÓ

XATÓ
ENDIVE AND FISH SALAD

Restaurants once served xató *only during the new wine season, but today this popular dish is available year round. It originally comes from the towns of Sitges, Vilanova and Vilafranca south-west of Barcelona. This delicate, rich salad is very refreshing in the late summer months. The name of the dish is said to come from a French artist, who is said to have exclaimed, 'Mais c'est un Château!' ('It's a castle!') when he was served this dish, piled high on its plate, some time in the late 19th century. Today, so-called* xatónades *are held in the region south-west of Barcelona, where chefs compete for awards for the best* xató *recipes.*

Serves 4 | **Preparation:** 10 minutes

INGREDIENTS

1 large head curly endive lettuce
16 anchovy fillets
400 g (14 oz) bacalao (salt cod),
    desalted, cut into bite-sized
    pieces
180 g (6 oz) can tuna
200 g (7 oz) olives, drained
    (preferably arbequina olives)
200 ml (7 fl oz) romesco sauce
    (see recipe on page 261)

PREPARATION

Divide the endive among four plates. Top with 4 anchovy fillets each, pieces of bacalao, tuna and olives. Serve drizzled with romesco sauce.

AMANIDA DE TOMÀQUET I ESPÀRRECS

ENSALADA TIBIA DE TOMATE Y ESPARRAGOS
WARM SALAD OF TOMATOES AND ASPARAGUS

The Baix Llobregat region produces tomatoes, parsley and a lot of green asparagus, so it isn't surprising to find a recipe combining these ingredients. This salad makes a vitamin-rich accompaniment to many summer dishes.

Serves 4 | **Preparation:** 20 minutes | **Cooking time:** 5 minutes

INGREDIENTS

1 bunch green asparagus

6 ripe tomatoes

Vinegar

Olive oil

1 pinch sugar

1 bunch flat-leaf (Italian) parsley

PREPARATION

Trim the hard asparagus ends from the asparagus and cut it into pieces about 4 cm (1½ inches) long. Blanch in boiling salted water until just cooked but still firm to the bite.

Meanwhile, cut the tomatoes into bite-sized pieces and toss with a vinaigrette of vinegar, olive oil, salt and sugar.

Pick off the parsley leaves from the stems. Chop coarsely and combine with the tomatoes and vinaigrette.

Drain the asparagus and immediately combine with the tomatoes. Season again to taste and serve warm.

CARGOLS A LA LLAUNA
CARACOLES A LA LLAUNA
BAKED SNAILS

Snails have always been and still are a nuisance in kitchen farmers' gardens, so something needs to be done about them. And what better solution could a true Catalan come up with if not to eat them? This recipe uses banded snails, which are a little smaller than the more expensive and more flavoursome Roman snails.

Serves 4 | **Preparation:** 20 minutes | **Baking time:** 20–25 minutes

INGREDIENTS

800 g (1 lb 12 oz) banded snails
   (ideally these should not have
   been fed for 1 week)

Coarse sea salt

Fine sea salt

3 garlic cloves

Olive oil

1 bunch curly parsley,
   very finely chopped

½ green capsicum (pepper)

Wine vinegar

Romesco sauce for drizzling
   (see recipe on page 261)

All i oli for dipping (see recipe
   on page 260)

PREPARATION

Preheat the oven to 180°C (350°F). Thoroughly wash the snails in cold water. Cover a baking tray with a layer of coarse sea salt about 3 mm (⅛ inch) thick. Spread the cleaned snails on top of the salt with the shell openings facing upwards. Sprinkle with a little fine salt. Cook on the middle rack of the oven for about 5 minutes.

Reduce the temperature to 160°C (320°F). Peel the garlic. Crush 2 cloves in a mortar and pestle together with a little olive oil and combine with two-thirds of the parsley. Drizzle this mixture over the snails and return the tray to the oven. Bake for another 5 minutes, then sprinkle with freshly ground black pepper and drizzle with olive oil. Return to the oven until the top of the snail meat has turned golden brown.

Meanwhile, finely dice the capsicum and the remaining garlic clove. Combine with olive oil, wine vinegar and a little parsley to make a vinaigrette.

Serve the cooked snails with toasted white bread, the vinaigrette, romesco sauce and *all i oli*, either straight from the baking tray or on a ceramic platter.

A different version of this recipe has the snails covered with about 500 g (1 lb 2 oz) very finely diced tomatoes and a little thyme before they are returned to the oven for the last time.

Many backyards in the old part of town are full of quiet, hidden corners that invite passers-by to have a break over a *caña*, a *copa* and some tapas.

The region around El Prat de Llobregat supplies Barcelona with fresh vegetables all year round, from delicate *calçots* (spring onions/scallions) early in the year to artichokes, broad beans, asparagus and lettuces throughout summer. Later in the year follow potatoes, of course, as well as eggplants (aubergines), tomatoes, capsicums (peppers) and a variety of legumes, all the way through to various cabbages in winter. This is a vegetarian's paradise!

Fish and seafood play a major role in Barcelona, and the seafood section of *La boquería* market has long been a tourist attraction. The variety of fish on offer is huge, as is the price difference between different types of fish. Aquaculture fish such as gilt-head bream and sea bass are cheap, but *peix de la platja*, that is, freshly caught fish, is at least three times as expensive. Still, both the superior quality and taste justify the higher price. Apart from widely known types of fish, you may also come across rarer varieties such as scorpion and weever fish, whose fins have poisonous barbs, which are trimmed off, though, before they are sold.

Poultry has always played an important role in Barcelonian cooking. The traditional regional cuisine works a lot with duck, and farmers in the Garraf district south-east of Barcelona even produce a DO-certified breed of chickens, *pollastre de pota blava*, as well as *pollastre del Penedès* nearby. Sure, the price for a single chicken is multiple times what you might pay for a take-away barbecued chicken, but a single bird will feed a whole family. And in Barcelona's traditional cuisine you'll come across so much more than just chicken: ducks, guinea fowl, partridges and quail also play an important culinary role.

MAIN DISHES

CALÇOTS
CALÇOTS
GRILLED SPRING ONIONS

Calçots *originally came from the region around Valls, about 60 kilometres south-west of Barcelona, but these days they are grown and enjoyed all around Barcelona and Tarragona. Local farmers tend to these special spring onions carefully for about a year and plant them tightly so they don't form much of a bulb and mainly greens instead.* Calçots *are available from December through to late spring. At least once a year, in spring, I simply have to have* calçots. *I love eating them casually from outdoor stalls with friends; in restaurants, they are often served with grilled meat and vegetables.*

Preparation: 30 minutes | **Resting time:** 10 minutes

INGREDIENTS

At least 10 *calçots* (spring onions/
  scallions) per person
Pork cutlets, lamb, blood pudding,
  butifarra
Sliced bread
Cannellini beans, artichokes
Plenty of romesco sauce
  (see recipe on page 261)

GRILL THE *CALÇOTS*, MAINS AND BREAD

Grill the *calçots* over an open fire, ideally made with old vine prunings, until the outer skin has blackened. Wrap in newspaper and set aside to rest for about 5–10 minutes.

Barbecue the meat for the main dish and toast the sliced bread on the remaining coals. This dish is commonly served in the form of a meat platter with blood pudding, pork cutlets and lamb, with cannellini beans and artichokes on the side.

ENJOY THE *CALÇOTS*

In Spain, grilled *calçots* are served on terracotta ridge tiles. To eat the *calçots*, carefully hold them at the green tops and peel off any blackened leaves in a downward motion. Dip the delicate, white portion of the bulb into the romesco sauce and eat it with your fingers. This is invariably a messy affair – it's best to toss aside any concerns and just enjoy the experience. Most restaurants hand out aprons to guests as they are served their *calçots*.

CARXOFES I PATATES EN VI BLANC
ALCACHOFAS I PATATAS AL VINO BIANCO
ARTICHOKES AND POTATOES IN WHITE WINE

Artichokes are all-rounders: They taste delicious both as a side dish and as a main.
This artichoke and potato stew is bound to be a favourite, not only among vegetarians.

Serves 4 | **Preparation:** 20 minutes | **Cooking time:** 45 minutes

INGREDIENTS

1 bottle of dry, fruity chardonnay
12 Spanish artichokes
12 potatoes
50 ml (1½ fl oz) olive oil
1 bay leaf
1 tablespoon dried thyme

PREPARE THE ARTICHOKES

Pour the wine into a bowl. Cut off and peel the artichoke stems and immediately drop them into the wine. Remove the artichoke petals, scrape the fibrous chokes from the hearts with a sharp-edged spoon and discard. Drop the hearts into the wine also to prevent oxidation.

COOK THE POTATOES AND ARTICHOKES

Peel the potatoes and cut them into eight chunks each. Heat a large casserole dish over medium heat. Add the olive oil, bay leaf, thyme, salt and freshly ground black pepper followed by the potato chunks and fry briefly. Stir in the wine from the bowl and add the artichoke hearts and stems. Simmer, half-covered, for about 20 minutes. Once the artichokes are done, remove them and set them aside.

Continue to cook the potatoes in the casserole dish, uncovered, until all of the liquid has evaporated. This will take about 20 minutes. Shake the dish occasionally to loosen the potatoes. They will firm up in the wine and retain their shape. Meanwhile, halve the artichoke hearts.

Return the artichoke hearts and stems to the dish once the remaining liquid begins to caramelise. Continue shaking the dish occasionally until the last drop of liquid has evaporated. Serve immediately.

CARXOFES AL FORN
ALCACHOFAS AL HORNO
BAKED ARTICHOKES

Barcelona and its surrounding region are well known for an incredible variety of artichoke dishes. The easiest way to prepare this wholesome, delicious vegetable is to roast it in the oven. Artichokes are quite filling; count one artichoke per person for a starter or three per person for a vegetarian main.

Serves 4 | **Preparation:** 10 minutes | **Baking time:** 1 hour

INGREDIENTS

4 oblong artichokes (or 12 if serving
  as a main meal)
1–2 garlic cloves, very thinly sliced
Plenty of olive oil
Romesco sauce (see recipe on
  page 261)

PREPARATION

Preheat the oven to 230°C (450°F). Trim off the artichoke stems so that they will stay upright in the roasting pan. Bash the artichoke heads once against the benchtop, stem side up, to loosen the petals a little.

Combine the garlic, olive oil, salt and freshly ground white pepper in a small bowl. Place the artichokes on a baking tray or in a roasting pan and pour some of the seasoned oil into the centre of each one. Transfer to the middle rack of the oven and reduce the temperature to 180°C (350°F). The artichokes will take about 45–60 minutes to cook through. Once done, the inner petals can be easily pulled out without taking much of the delicate heart with them.

Artichokes match particularly well with romesco sauce. Pull out the petals, one by one, dip the fleshy part into the sauce and pull the petal through the teeth. Make sure you remove the fibrous chokes before eating the delicate artichoke hearts.

TARTA DE CARXOFES AMB PATATES

PASTEL DE ALCACHOFAS Y PATATAS
ARTICHOKE AND POTATO GRATIN

*This recipe for oven-baked Spanish artichokes with potatoes is a hearty, rustic affair
that will delight the hearts and palates of all fans of this exquisite vegetable.*

Serves 4–6 | **Preparation:** 25 minutes | **Cooking and baking time:** 1¼ hours

INGREDIENTS

12 artichokes

Juice of 1 lemon

1.5 kg (3 lb 5 oz) waxy potatoes

1 tablespoon olive oil, plus some
extra for the tin

1 large onion, diced

1 bunch flat-leaf (Italian) parsley,
chopped

4 sage leaves, thinly sliced

250 g (9 oz) crème fraîche

2 eggs

200 g (7 oz) grated cheese
(e.g. emmental)

COOK THE ARTICHOKES AND POTATOES

Cut off and peel the artichoke stems and immediately drop them into a bowl of water
with the lemon juice added. Pick off the artichoke petals until you get to the choke and
heart. Scrape and discard the fibrous chokes from the hearts with a sharp-edged spoon
and immediately drop the hearts into the acidulated water.

Cook the artichoke hearts and stems in salted water for 10–12 minutes, then remove
from the cooking liquid and refresh under cold water. Slice the artichoke hearts.

Peel and slice the potatoes. Blanch the potatoes in a pot of boiling salted water for
about 5 minutes, then refresh under cold water and drain. Heat a little olive oil in a
frying pan over medium heat and briefly sauté the onion.

PREPARE AND BAKE THE GRATIN

Combine the artichoke hearts and stems with the onion, parsley, sage, crème fraîche,
eggs and cheese in a bowl. Season with salt and freshly ground black pepper.

Preheat the oven to 180°C (350°F). Brush a springform tin with olive oil. Layer
half of the sliced potatoes to cover the bottom and side of the tin. Cover with half of
the artichoke and egg mixture, then add another layer of potato and finish with the
remaining artichoke and egg mixture. Bake on the middle rack of the preheated oven
for 50 minutes. Remove from the oven and leave to cool on a cooling rack. Remove
the gratin from the tin and serve. This gratin is delicious served with a rocket (arugula)
salad dressed with a herb vinaigrette.

ALBERGÍNES FARCIDAS

BERENJENAS RELLENAS
STUFFED EGGPLANTS

The district of Baix Llobregat south-west of Barcelona is the city's kitchen garden. It produces not only broad beans and artichokes, but also excellent tomatoes and eggplants. Eggplants are another vegetable that can be prepared in a thousand and one ways. These stuffed eggplants are one of my favourite dishes, but unfortunately they have fallen a little out of fashion, even though they are very easy to prepare.

Serves 4 | **Preparation:** 15 minutes | **Cooking and baking time:** 40 minutes

INGREDIENTS

4 large eggplants (aubergines)

1 tablespoon olive oil

1 small red capsicum (pepper), finely diced

300 g (10½ oz) mixed minced (ground) meat

1 onion, finely diced

1 large, ripe tomato, diced

½ teaspoon ground cinnamon

Freshly ground nutmeg

1 tablespoon mild paprika

200 g (7 oz) grated emmental cheese

PREPARE THE EGGPLANTS

Preheat the oven to 180°C (350°F). Halve the eggplants lengthwise, leaving the stem base intact, and score the flesh in a diamond pattern. Place the eggplant halves in an ovenproof dish, cut side up, and bake on the middle rack of the preheated oven for 20 minutes. Remove from the oven and carefully scoop out the flesh, making sure the skin remains intact.

Transfer the eggplant flesh to a bowl, mash coarsely and set aside. Reduce the oven temperature to 150°C (300°F).

PREPARE THE FILLING AND BAKE THE EGGPLANT

Heat a little olive oil in a frying pan over medium heat and sear the capsicum. Once it begins to soften, add the minced meat and onion. Continue to fry until browned. Add the tomato and season with cinnamon, nutmeg, paprika, salt and freshly ground black pepper. Simmer until almost all of the liquid has evaporated, then fold in the mashed eggplant flesh.

Fill the eggplant halves with the minced meat mixture and sprinkle with the cheese. Bake on the middle rack of the oven for 10–15 minutes until the cheese is golden brown and bubbling.

ALBERGÍNES AMB TORTA DEL CASAR

BERENJENAS CON TORTA DEL CASAR
BAKED EGGPLANTS WITH TORTA DEL CASAR

Spain has relatively few types of unpasteurised cheese that have real character, but one of them is Torta del Casar from the Extremadura region. This cheese turns very soft as it matures and is then scooped out of the wheel with spoons. I was once served this cheese in Barcelona as part of the dish in the recipe below, which I find thoroughly delectable.

Serves 4 | **Preparation:** 10 minutes | **Frying and baking time:** 15 minutes

INGREDIENTS

4 medium-sized, relatively slender
   eggplants (aubergines)
1 tablespoon olive oil
1 Torta del Casar (from specialist
   suppliers or ordered online;
   alternatively another full-
   flavoured soft cheese, e.g.
   Epoisses de Bourgogne)
4 slices of white bread, toasted

PREPARATION

Preheat the oven to 180°C (350°F). Trim the stem bases off the eggplants and quarter the vegetables lengthwise. Halve the quarters again. Sprinkle the eggplant pieces with a little salt and set them aside to draw out some of their moisture. Pat dry. Heat an ovenproof pan over high heat and briefly sear the eggplant pieces in the olive oil, then transfer to the oven and cook until done.

Have a ripe Torta del Casar ready at room temperature. Score the top crosswise and then fold back the top segments. Serve the eggplant, cheese and toasts on a platter with a spoon for the cheese.

FAVES A LA CATALANA
HABAS A LA CATALANA
CATALAN BROAD BEANS

Broad beans are among the oldest legumes in European cooking, and apparently even the Ancient Egyptians relied on them in their diet. They are also a staple of traditional Spanish cuisine. The Baix Llobregat region produces habas *and* faves *of the highest quality. As just about anything else, broad beans also taste best fresh. If you prefer your culinary adventures to be effortless, simply buy broad beans shelled and ready to cook so you don't have to shell them yourself. This is more expensive, of course, but luckily broad beans are also available canned or frozen. This is a very typical Barcelonian dish that proves yet again that hearty home cooking is often among the very best.*

Serves 4 | **Preparation:** 10 minutes | **Cooking time:** 1 hour 25 minutes

INGREDIENTS

1 dash olive oil

100 g (3½ oz) thickly sliced smoked ham, coarsely chopped

1 garlic clove, crushed

1 slice serrano ham or other dry-cured ham

1 onion, finely diced

1 small sprig rosemary

2 bay leaves

3 ripe tomatoes, seeded and coarsely diced

50 ml (1½ fl oz) dry sherry or dry red wine

1 tablespoon aniseed spirit

750 g (1 lb 10 oz) fresh shelled or canned broad beans

1 large sprig mint

100 ml (3½ fl oz) meat stock

100 g (3½ oz) botifarra blanca or another sausage for frying

100 g (3½ oz) botifarra negra or a mild black pudding

PREPARATION

Heat the olive oil in a deep frying pan over high heat and fry the smoked ham and garlic until golden brown. Add the serrano ham and onion and continue to fry, stirring. Add the rosemary and bay leaves and fry for another 3–4 minutes.

Stir in the tomatoes, cover and simmer for 7–8 minutes. Add the sherry and aniseed spirit, then lower the heat and simmer until the sauce reduces and gradually darkens in colour. Fold in the broad beans and torn mint leaves. Add enough stock and water to just cover everything. Season with salt and braise over low heat for 40 minutes.

Slice the sausages 1 cm (½ inch) thick and add to the sauce. Season again with salt and cook, uncovered, for another 15–20 minutes. Remove the herb sprigs and serve in a warmed ceramic bowl.

ESPINACS A LA CATALANA
ESPINACAS A LA CATALANA
SPINACH WITH RAISINS AND PINE NUTS

Espinacs a la catalana, *spinach with raisins and pine nuts, is a true culinary winner. In some restaurants, this delicious dish is also served under the name of* espinacs con pasas y piñones.

Serves 4 | **Preparation:** 10 minutes | **Cooking time:** 15 minutes

INGREDIENTS

2 tablespons raisins, soaked
    in water
750 g (1 lb 10 oz) baby English
    spinach
4 tablespoons olive oil
2 tablespoons pine nuts
1 small garlic clove, halved

PREPARATION

Drain the raisins. Wash and drain the baby spinach. Transfer the damp leaves to a large pot and cover with a lid. Cook over high heat for 2–3 minutes until the spinach has collapsed. Leave to cool, then squeeze out the excess moisture and chop finely.

Heat a large pan over medium heat. Add the olive oil, pine nuts and garlic and fry until the nuts start to colour. Shake the pan frequently to prevent them from burning. Remove the garlic. Add the raisins and spinach to the pan. Season with salt and freshly ground black pepper and continue to fry for another 5 minutes, stirring occasionally. Serve straight from the pan or on small plates. Serve with ham and bread.

TIP

You can, of course, also use frozen spinach for this dish. Simply defrost before using and cook in a little water for a few minutes to soften.

MARKETS

In Barcelona, each quarter has its own market. These markets are where locals shop for fresh fruit and vegetables, fish, poultry and meat, above all. Generally, restaurant chefs are the first to do their shopping in the early mornings. A little later, it's local housewives, and by late morning the markets are flooded with tourists.

Barcelona's most famous market is definitely the Mercat de Sant Josep, better known as *La boquería*, which is renowned for its excellent seafood section. However, more and more stalls on *La boquería* are focusing squarely on tourists, and the market has lost a lot of its inimitable flair as a result – enough to have people thinking aloud about limiting tourist numbers.

A number of the city's other markets have been extensively refurbished or are currently undergoing refurbishment. The Mercat de Santa Caterina in the Born/La Ribera quarter, for example, was completed in 2005, and the Mercat Ninot, which serves the Eixample quarter, in 2015. One of Barcelona's most beautiful markets, the Mercat de Sant Antoni, is currently being restored.

CIGRONS AMB CLOÏSSES

GARBANZOS CON ALMEJAS
CHICKPEAS WITH CLAMS

*Chickpeas are incredibly versatile legumes that have found their way into kitchens all
over the world, and quite rightly so, as they are both delicious and healthy. People all around
the Mediterranean recognised their excellent culinary value early on and created a great variety
of chickpea recipes. In Spain, pre-cooked chickpeas are available in bulk from butchers,
or people simply buy them canned from supermarkets.*

Serves 4 | **Preparation:** 10 minutes | **Cooking time:** 35 minutes | **Soaking time:** 4–5 hours

INGREDIENTS

250 g (9 oz) clams (vongole)

Olive oil for frying

1 small garlic clove, crushed

½ teaspoon cayenne pepper

1 onion, diced

2 carrots, diced

1 pinch sweet paprika

1 tablespoon plain (all-purpose)
    flour

1 small glass white wine

300 g (10½ oz) canned chickpeas,
    drained

500 ml (17 fl oz) vegetable stock

Flat-leaf (Italian) parsley, chopped,
    for garnish

Chives, chopped, for garnish

1 small red chilli, sliced into rings

PREPARATION

Place the clams in cold salted water – use 50 g (1¾ oz) salt per 1 litre (35 fl oz) water) –
for 4–5 hours to make sure they excrete any sand and other impurities.

Heat a large pan over medium heat. Add the olive oil and garlic and fry gently. As
soon as the garlic starts to colour, season with cayenne pepper and add the onion and
carrots. Cook until the vegetables are soft, about 10 minutes, then dust with paprika
and flour. Deglaze with the wine and allow some of the liquid to evaporate. Add the
chickpeas and vegetable stock. Simmer again for a few minutes until almost all of
the liquid has been absorbed by the chickpeas.

Heat another pan over high heat. Add olive oil and the drained clams, cover and
cook until the clams have opened. Discard any clams that remain closed.

Add the clams to the vegetables, simmer everything for another 5 minutes and
season with salt and freshly ground black pepper. Sprinkle with some parsley, chives
and chilli for garnish and serve.

AMANIDA DE CIGRONS
GARBANZOS ALIÑADOS
CHICKPEA SALAD

Cooked chickpeas are incredibly versatile: they are excellent in warming stews or as a side dish,
and cold chickpeas provide a substantial and delicious base for refreshing summer salads.

Serves 4 | **Preparation:** 15 minutes

INGREDIENTS

1 mild onion, finely diced

1 Lebanese (short) cucumber,
  peeled and finely diced

1 green or red capsicum (pepper),
  seeded and finely diced

1 carrot, cooked, finely diced

1 hard-boiled egg, finely diced

500 g (1 lb 2 oz) canned chickpeas,
  drained

240 g (8½ oz) can corn, drained

Vinegar

Olive oil

PREPARATION

Combine the onion, cucumber, capsicum, carrot and egg in a large bowl and fold
in the chickpeas and corn. Dress the salad with a vinaigrette prepared from vinegar,
olive oil and salt.

TIP

Chickpeas taste even better if they are freshly cooked. Soak dried chickpeas overnight
in plenty of water with a little added bicarbonate of soda (baking soda) for 24 hours.
(As a guide, use 1 tablespoon bicarbonate of soda per 300 g/10½ oz dried chickpeas.)
The next day, boil the soaked chickpeas for about 1 hour, skimming off any scum
forming on the surface. Drain well before use.

POTATGE DE CIGRONS AMB CHORIZO
POTAJE DE GARBANZOS CON CHORIZO
CHICKPEA STEW WITH CHORIZO

This stew is eaten all over Spain, with varying ingredients,
but I prefer this particularly hearty recipe over any others.

Serves 4 | **Preparation:** 10 minutes | **Frying and cooking time:** 30 minutes

INGREDIENTS

Olive oil for frying

200 g (7 oz) chorizo, sliced

1 garlic clove, crushed

1 onion, chopped

1 carrot, sliced

1 red capsicum (pepper), diced

1 green capsicum (pepper), diced

600 g (1 lb 5 oz) canned chickpeas,
   drained

1 potato, finely diced

1 tomato, peeled, seeded and
   finely diced

1–3 bay leaves

PREPARATION

Heat a large saucepan over medium heat, add the olive oil and fry the sliced chorizo. If the chorizo releases a lot of oil, skim some off. Add the garlic and fry briefly, then add the onion, carrot and capsicums. Cook over low heat until soft, then season with salt and freshly ground black pepper. Add water until it comes up about 2 fingers wide. Bring to the boil, add the chickpeas and increase the heat again.

   As soon as the stew returns to the boil, add the potato, tomato and bay leaves. Increase the heat to high and cover to return to the boil, then reduce the heat again and simmer until the potato and chickpeas are cooked through. Season once more with salt and serve.

MONGETES SEQUES AMB BOTIFARRA
ALUBIAS CON BUTIFARRA
BEANS WITH BOTIFARRA

Common beans were introduced to Catalonia in the 16th century and soon became a very popular crop. They could be cooked fresh and, more importantly, could also be dried and stored over extended periods. Botifarra is a type of fresh sausage for frying, which has a high content of lean meat, often even fillet meat. The earliest written record of this very popular dish dates back to 1830. The sausages taste even better barbecued; in this case, simply fry the beans in olive oil with a little diced bacon.

Serves 4 | **Preparation:** 10 minutes | **Cooking time:** 15 minutes

INGREDIENTS
4 fresh botifarra sausages
Olive oil for frying
600 g (1 lb 5 oz) canned cannellini
    beans, drained

For the *picada*
Flat-leaf (Italian) parsley, finely
    chopped
1 garlic clove, crushed
Olive oil

FRY THE SAUSAGES AND BEANS
Prick the sausages with a fork all over to prevent them from bursting while you fry them. Sear the sausages in olive oil in a large pan over high heat. Reduce the heat to cook the sausages until done. Remove them from the pan, reserving the fat in the pan, and keep them warm.

Fry the beans in the reserved fat over high heat until they start to colour. Season with salt and freshly ground black pepper. Return the sausages to the pan for the last few minutes of cooking to reheat.

PREPARE A *PICADA*
Combine the parsley and garlic with a little olive oil to make a *picada* sauce. Drizzle the sauce over the beans to serve.

NCES

9.90 € Quilo.

HAVARTI BARRA
Especial sandwich
Sabor: suau.
Llet: vaca.
Origen: Dinamarca.
Mat. Grasa: 60% 9.90 € Quilo

♥ Sólo 6% de Grasa Saturada
♥ 75% menos de Colesterol
♥ Sin Lactosa
♥ Sin Gluten
TRENTA
GOUDA VEGETAL. SENSE LACTOSA
16.90 € Quilo

GOUDA TENDRE
Sabor: Suau.
Llet: Vaca.
Origen: Holanda.
Mat. Grasa: 45% 8.90 € Quilo

BOLA SEMI-SEC
Sabor: Gustós.
Llet: Vaca.
Origen: Holanda.
Mat. Grasa: 45% 10.90 € Quilo

BOLA SEC
Sabor: Intens
Llet: Vaca.
Origen: Holanda.
Mat. Grasa 45% 11.90 € Quilo

BOLA TENDRE
Sabor: Suau.
Llet: Vaca.
Origen: Holanda.
Grasa: 45% 8.90 € Quilo

MANTEGA DEL CADI
Absolutament pura
11.90 € Quilo

EntreMont

You won't find the enormous variety of cheeses in Barcelona that you have in Paris, but it's worth scouting local shops and markets for some cheese specialties in addition to standard varieties.

PATATES I SOBRASSADA
PATATAS Y SOBRASSADA
MASHED POTATOES WITH SOBRASSADA

Potatoes with sobrassada originated as a peasant dish from Mallorca.
Sobrassada is a typically Mallorcan spreadable sausage made out of smoked pork.
I was once served this dish, prepared particularly exquisitely, as a first course in the
'La Semproniana' restaurant, and I love cooking it as a surprise for my guests at home.

Serves 4 | **Preparation:** 15 minutes | **Cooking time:** 25 minutes

INGREDIENTS

800 g (1 lb 12 oz) floury potatoes

150–200 ml (5–7 fl oz) lukewarm milk

40 g (1½ oz) butter

Freshly ground nutmeg

1 tablespoon finely chopped herbs
to taste, such as basil, flat-leaf
(Italian) parsley and coriander
(cilantro)

200 ml (7 fl oz) cream

150 g (5½ oz) parmesan cheese,
grated

4 slices sobrassada, skin removed,
about 2 cm (¾ inch) thick and
6 cm (2½ inches) in diameter

Left-over gravy to taste

PREPARE THE MASHED POTATOES AND SAUCE

Peel the potatoes and boil them in salted water. Drain and combine them with the milk, butter and a pinch of nutmeg. Coarsely mash, fold in the herbs and keep warm.

Heat the cream in a small saucepan over low heat. Add the parmesan to melt.

PUT TOGETHER THE STACKS

Place four 9 cm (3½ inch) ring moulds onto plates and half fill them with hot mashed potatoes. Top with 1 slice sof obrassada each and divide the remaining mashed potatoes among the stacks. Remove the ring moulds and pierce the stacks along the sides at the level of the sobrassada so that its melting red fat drains decoratively onto the plate.

Pour a bed of parmesan sauce around the stack and drizzle the stack with the sauce. If you have any left-over gravy from the day before, use it for garnish. Season with a little grated nutmeg.

NÍSCALOS AMB ALL I JULIVERT

ROVELLONES CON AJO Y PEREJIL
RED PINE MUSHROOMS WITH GARLIC AND PARSLEY

In Catalonia, the mushroom season starts some time in late summer, depending on the weather. The region's most highly coveted mushrooms are definitely rovellones *or* níscalos, *that is, red pine mushrooms, which are prepared in any number of creative ways. This simple recipe really brings out their unique flavour.*

Serves 4 | **Preparation:** 5 minutes | **Cooking time:** 10 minutes

INGREDIENTS

800 g (1 lb 12 oz) red pine
    mushrooms (ideally small ones)
1 small garlic clove
2 tablespoons flat-leaf (Italian)
    parsley leaves
1 small sprig rosemary
4 tablespoons olive oil
Sea salt flakes

PREPARATION

Clean the mushrooms with a brush and a damp tea towel. Peel the garlic and chop coarsely, together with the parsley and a few rosemary leaves.

Heat the olive oil in a frying pan over medium heat. Add the mushrooms, fry and season lightly with sea salt. Add the herb mixture once the mushrooms start to colour but are still firm to the bite. Continue to fry briefly. Serve with white bread.

OUS FREGITS AMB OU DE REIG
HUEVOS FRITOS CON ORONJA
FRIED EGGS WITH CAESAR'S MUSHROOMS

In Catalonia, Caesar's mushrooms, ou de reig, *are the undisputed 'kings of mushrooms'. Caesar's mushrooms (*Amanita caesarea*) belong to the death cap family, but they are edible, very much in contrast to most of their relatives. Unfortunately they are not commonly available in stores, despite being among the best edible mushrooms around. If you ever find Caesar's mushrooms on a menu, make sure not to miss the experience. I was once lucky enough to enjoy them in a very simple, yet truly regal and exquisitely delicious dish served at the 'Dos Cielos' restaurant in Barcelona: fried eggs with Caesar's mushrooms.*

Serves 4 | **Preparation:** 10 minutes | **Cooking time:** 15 minutes

INGREDIENTS
400 g (14 oz) Caesar's mushrooms
Olive oil for frying
60 g (2¼ oz) French shallots,
    finely diced
50 ml (1½ fl oz) chicken stock
8 eggs
Shaved manchego cheese
Chopped chives

PREPARATION
Clean the mushrooms with a brush and a damp tea towel. If the mushrooms are large, peel off their orange skins and halve them. If the caps are still closed, only remove the white outer skin and also halve the mushrooms.

Heat a little olive oil in a frying pan over medium heat and sauté the shallots. Add the mushrooms and chicken stock. Season with salt and freshly ground black pepper and sauté for a few minutes to reduce the liquid somewhat.

Meanwhile, prepare the fried eggs in another pan, making sure that the egg yolks remain runny. Transfer 2 fried eggs onto each plate and season with salt and pepper. Top with the cooked mushrooms. Garnish with shaved manchego cheese and chives and drizzle with the bright yellow mushroom juices from the pan.

RAVIOLI DE BOLETS
RAVIOLI DE SETAS
MUSHROOM RAVIOLI

Lorenç Patràs' market stall is right at the front of La boquería *market. In Barcelona, Lorenç is THE expert for anything to do with mushrooms, and his stall is where most restaurants and mushroom aficionados do their shopping. Lorenç organises a private cooking competition among his customers every year, and this winning recipe astounded even him.*

Serves 4 | **Preparation:** 30 minutes | **Frying and cook ing time:** 20 minutes

INGREDIENTS

1 kg (2 lb 4 oz) mixed mushrooms
   (chanterelles, black chanterelles,
   red pine mushrooms etc.)
Olive oil for frying
1 small garlic clove, chopped
1 small piece fresh ginger, about
   4 cm (1½ inches), finely minced
4–5 sage leaves, thinly sliced
1 chorizo criollo sausage,
   skin removed
1 egg
Breadcrumbs
4 tablespoons grated parmesan
   cheese
Plain (all-purpose) flour for dusting
300 g (10½ oz) pasta dough, made
   from durum wheat semolina
60 g (2¼ oz) butter
Flat-leaf (Italian) parsley for garnish

PREPARE THE FILLING

Clean the mushrooms with a brush and a damp tea towel and coarsely chop. Heat the olive oil in a large pan or a wok over medium heat. Add the chopped garlic and fry until golden brown, but be careful not to burn it. Add the ginger and mushrooms. Season with three-quarters of the sage and a little salt. Allow any liquid to evaporate. Remove the pan from the heat and set aside to cool. Remove the mushroom mixture from the pan and chop finely. Set aside a quarter of the mushroom mixture.

Shred or chop the sausage and fry in the same pan over medium heat. Transfer to a bowl and add the remaining mushroom mixture, egg, some breadcrumbs and half the parmesan. Mix to combine.

PREPARE THE RAVIOLI

Dust your workbench with flour and roll out the pasta dough into two thin sheets.

Use a tablespoon to divide the filling across one of the pasta sheets, leaving about 6 cm (2½ inches) in between portions. Moisten the dough with water around the filling and place the second sheet on top. Press the two pasta sheets together firmly around the filling. Use a pizza cutter to cut the dough into individual ravioli.

Boil the ravioli in salted water for 3 minutes. They are done as soon as they rise to the top. Drain, divide among serving plates and keep warm.

Gently heat the reserved mushroom mixture in a frying pan with the butter and remaining sage. Divide among the plates with the ravioli. Sprinkle with the remaining parmesan and the parsley and serve.

LLUÇ AMB VERDURETES
I OLI DE FONOLL

MERLUZA CON VERDURA Y ACEITE DE HINOJO Y LIMÓN
HAKE WITH JULIENNED VEGETABLES AND HERB OIL

To me, lluç *or* merluza, *that is, hake, tends to be quite boring compared to other fish.*
But served with fennel, as in this recipe, it suddenly becomes quite exciting.

Serves 4 | **Preparation:** 20 minutes | **Cooking time:** 15 minutes

INGREDIENTS
For the herb oil

½ bulb fennel, with fronds

3–4 sprigs dill

4–5 sprigs parsley

½ lemon

1 small cup of olive oil

1 pinch sugar

For the fish fillets

4 hake fillets

Olive oil for frying

For the julienned vegetables

1 eggplant (aubergine)

1 green capsicum (pepper)

1 zucchini (courgette)

1 carrot

Olive oil for frying

½ sprig rosemary, leaves
   picked off

1 onion, cut into thick rounds

PREPARE THE HERB OIL

Thinly slice the fennel and most of the fronds. Finely chop the dill and parsley. Zest and juice the lemon. Whisk the herbs, lemon zest, a little of the lemon juice and olive oil to a dressing in a bowl. Toss with the fennel and season with sugar and freshly ground black pepper. Leave to marinate at room temperature.

FRY THE HAKE FILLETS

Briefly sear the hake fillets in olive oil in a pan over high heat, flesh side down. Flip over and cook on the skin side. Season with a little salt.

FRY THE JULIENNED VEGETABLES

Wash and trim the eggplant, capsicum, zucchini and carrot. Cut into julienne strips about 5 mm (¼ inch) thick and 4 cm (1½ inches) long. Heat a little olive oil in a pan over high heat and fry the vegetable strips until cooked but still firm to the bite. Season with a little salt and rosemary, then remove from the pan. Fry the onion slices in a little olive oil.

Divide the hake fillets among warmed plates, top with the julienned vegetables and drizzle the fish with the herb oil. Arrange the onion rounds on the side and serve.

LLOBARRO AMB MERMELATA DE CEBA

LUBINA CON MERMELADA DE CEBOLLA
SEA BASS WITH ONION JAM

Freshly caught llobarro *or* lubina, *that is, sea bass, is one of the tastiest fish found in the Mediterranean, as its firm, aromatic flesh makes it a true delicacy. The fillets of a large sea bass, cut horizontally across the back, taste best. The sweetness of the onion jam harmonises fantastically with this aromatic fish, making for an exquisite, yet simple, dish.*

Serves 2 | **Preparation:** 10 minutes | **Cooking time:** 15 minutes

INGREDIENTS

For the onion jam
Olive oil for frying
6 large onions, halved and sliced
1 pinch salt
1 tablespoon honey

For the fish fillets
2 large sea bass fillets
Olive oil for frying

PREPARE THE ONION JAM
For the onion jam, heat the olive oil in a large pan over medium heat. Add the onions, fry and season with salt. Add the honey and keep frying until the onions soften and brown. Keep warm.

FRY THE SEA BASS FILLETS
Pat the fish fillets dry and season lightly with salt and freshly ground black pepper. Heat the olive oil over medium heat in another pan. Briefly sear the fish fillets, flesh side first, then flip over and cook on the skin side.

Arrange the onion jam on top of the fish fillets. Serve with a tomato salad.

RAP A LA MARINERA
RAPE A LA MARINERA
MONKFISH A LA MARINERA

Monkfish look rather grim, despite their name, which would suggest a somewhat more rarefied appearance. However, their boneless, delicate flesh is a sheer delight, and chefs all over Barcelona have come up with a range of highly inventive recipes for preparing this specialty.

Serves 4 | **Preparation:** 25 minutes | **Frying and cooking time:** 40 minutes

INGREDIENTS

Olive oil for frying

1 onion, finely diced

1 garlic clove, thinly sliced

1 red chilli, seeded and minced

1 slice white bread, toasted
and diced

12 blanched almonds, finely
chopped

4–5 sprigs flat-leaf (Italian) parsley,
coarsely chopped

125 ml (4 fl oz) white wine

250 ml (9 fl oz) fish stock (see recipe
on page 261)

6 monkfish or rocklobster fillets,
about 125 g (4½ oz) each

Plain (all-purpose) flour for dusting

4 prawns (shrimp)

4 crayfish

PREPARATION

Heat the olive oil in a frying pan over high heat. Add the onion, garlic and chilli and sear briefly. Stir in the diced bread, almonds and most of the parsley. Add the white wine and bring everything to the boil. Blend using a stick blender, add the fish stock and briefly return to the boil. Take off the heat and keep warm.

Preheat the oven to 155°C (310°F). Wash the fish, pat dry and season with salt and freshly ground black pepper. Dust the fish fillets in flour and briefly sear in olive oil over medium heat on both sides. Transfer to an ovenproof dish, drizzle with the hot oil from the pan and bake on the middle rack of the preheated oven for 10–15 minutes.

Fry the prawns and crayfish in olive oil for 10 minutes. Arrange on plates together with the fish and the sauce. Garnish with parsley and serve.

BACALAO A LA LLAUNA
BACALAO A LA LLAUNA
BAKED BACALAO

This bacalao recipe, which is very typically Catalan, and particularly Barcelonian, is named after the dish in which it is traditionally prepared. A llauna *is a zinc-coated steel dish about 25 cm (10 inches) square and 4 cm (1½ inches) deep, with handles, that was often used for cooking over open fires. These days,* bacalao a la llauna *is most commonly cooked in a clay casserole dish in a standard oven.*

Serves 4–6 | **Preparation:** 10 minutes | **Frying and baking time:** 35 minutes

INGREDIENTS

800 g (1 lb 12 oz) bacalao (salt cod), desalted, without skin or bones

50 g (1¾ oz) plain (all-purpose) flour

200 ml (7 fl oz) olive oil

3 garlic cloves, thinly sliced

1 tablespoon sweet paprika

1 glass white wine

PREPARATION

Preheat the oven to 160°C (320°F). Cut the bacalao into even pieces and dust these in the flour. Heat the olive oil in a frying pan over high heat. Add the fish and sear for 2–3 minutes on each side. Remove from the pan, drain on paper towel and transfer to a clay baking dish.

Fry the garlic in the pan until golden brown. Remove the pan from the heat and stir in the paprika and white wine. Return to medium heat, simmer to reduce, then drizzle the bacalao with the thickened sauce. Transfer to the middle rack of the preheated oven and cook for about 15 minutes until cooked through. Serve with a side salad, cannellini beans or potatoes.

BACALAO AMB CEBA I MEL AL FORN

BACALAO CON CEBOLLA Y MIEL AL HORNO
BAKED BACALAO WITH HONEY AND ONIONS

Honey harmonises perfectly with the salt in the bacalao to deliver a delicately balanced flavour.
There is another version of this recipe, where the fish is served with sweet apples.

Serves 4–6 | **Preparation:** 10 minutes | **Frying and baking time:** 35 minutes

INGREDIENTS

50 ml (1½ fl oz) olive oil

3–4 onions, sliced

1 small garlic clove, crushed

2 tablespoons honey

1 kg (2 lb 4 oz) bacalao (salt cod),
    desalted, without skin or bones,
    cut into 4–6 pieces

2 tablespoons plain (all-purpose)
    flour, plus extra for dusting

40 g (1½ oz) butter

250 ml (9 fl oz) milk

1 pinch freshly ground nutmeg

CARAMELISE THE ONIONS

Heat half of the olive oil in a frying pan over medium heat. Add the onions and garlic to sauté. Season lightly with salt. Once the onions start to colour, stir in the honey and caramelise everything for a few minutes.

FRY AND BAKE THE BACALAO

Dust the bacalao in flour and fry over high heat for 2 minutes on each side. Remove from the pan and set aside to drain on paper towel.

Transfer the bacalao to a clay baking dish. Preheat the oven to 180°C (350°F). Prepare a béchamel sauce from the butter, 2 tablespoons flour and milk, season with a little salt and nutmeg and pour on top of the bacalao. Place the baking dish in the oven and immediately reduce the temperature to 150°C (300°F). Bake until done, about 20 minutes. Serve with mashed potatoes and the caramelised onions.

BACALAO AMB SAMFAINA
BACALAO CON SAMFAINA
BACALAO WITH SAMFAINA

Bacalao and samfaina are two very traditional ingredients of Barcelonian cooking.
Combined in a clay dish, they make an excellent pairing of flavours.

Serves 4 | **Preparation:** 15 minutes | **Frying and baking time:** 25 minutes

INGREDIENTS

500 g (1 lb 2 oz) bacalao (salt cod),
   desalted, without skin or bones

3 tablespoons plain (all-purpose)
   flour

Olive oil for frying

2 onions, finely diced

2 garlic cloves, crushed

1 red capsicum (pepper),
   finely diced

1 green capsicum (pepper),
   finely diced

1 large eggplant (aubergine),
   finely diced

2 small zucchini (courgettes),
   finely diced

2 ripe tomatoes, peeled and
   finely diced

Sugar

PREPARE THE BACALAO AND VEGETABLES

Pat the bacalao dry and cut into several small pieces. Dust with flour and fry in olive oil over medium heat until golden brown. Remove from the pan and drain on paper towel.

Add the onions, garlic and capsicums to the same pan, plus extra olive oil if needed, and fry for 5 minutes. Stir in the remaining vegetables and sauté briefly. Deglaze with a little water and season with salt, freshly ground black pepper and sugar.

Return the fish pieces to the pan and cook with the vegetables until everything is done, about 5–10 minutes. Add more water or some fish stock if the pan gets too dry.

Divide the bacalao and samfaina among plates and serve.

LLOBARRO AL FORN AL ESTIL PESCADER

LUBINA AL HORNO AL ESTILO PESCADOR
BAKED SEA BASS, FISHERMAN'S STYLE

Oven-baking is a very traditional way of preparing fish in Barcelona.
The fish best suited for this type of cooking are gilt-head bream and sea bass.

Serves 4 | **Preparation:** 15 minutes | **Frying and baking time:** 35 minutes

INGREDIENTS

1 kg (2 lb 4 oz) potatoes, peeled
   and sliced

1 onion, thinly sliced

1 bay leaf

200 ml (7 fl oz) olive oil

200 g (7 oz) tomatoes, quartered

1 glass white wine

2 sea bass or gilt-head bream,
   about 1 kg (2 lb 4 oz) each,
   kitchen-ready (or 4 fillets)

1 red chilli, thinly sliced into rings

2 garlic cloves, thinly sliced

2 tablespoons vinegar

BAKE THE FISH

Preheat the oven to 160°C (320°F). Place the potatoes, onion and bay leaf into a large baking dish and season with salt and freshly ground black pepper. Drizzle with 100 ml (3½ fl oz) of the olive oil and put on the middle rack of the oven. Once the potatoes are partially cooked after about 10–15 minutes, add the tomatoes and pour in the white wine. Return to the oven and cook until done.

Lightly sear the fish in a non-stick pan over medium heat. Place the fish on top of the baked vegetables and continue to cook in the oven until done.

PREPARE THE SAUCE

For the sauce, heat the remaining olive oil in a pan over medium heat. Add the chilli and garlic and fry until golden brown, then stir in the vinegar. Arrange the fish and vegetables on plates and drizzle with the sauce.

CALAMARSET
CHIPIRON
14,30
P.V.P. €UROS KILO

XANGUET
CHANQUETE
20,50
€UROS KILO

CAN̤AILLA
CAN̤AILLA

PROHIBIDO
FUMAR

RESERVAT EL DRET
D'ADMISSIÓ

People often queue happily for a table at 'La Paradeta'. Its food comes straight from the market stall into the kitchen.

SALMONETES A LA PARILLA

SALMONETES A LA PARILLA
GRILLED RED MULLET

*Both striped red mullet (moll/salmonete de roca) and red mullet (moll/salmonete de fang)
are sold at the city's markets, and both are used in a similar manner in Catalan cooking,
but striped red mullet is the somewhat preferred fish.*

Serves 4 | **Preparation:** 10 minutes | **Grilling time:** 5 minutes

INGREDIENTS

8 kitchen-ready red mullets
16 sprigs rosemary
2 lemons, halved lengthwise
   and sliced
Olive oil for basting
Coarse sea salt

PREPARATION

Preheat the oven on the grill (broiler) setting. Score the skin of each fish several times. Season with salt and stuff with a rosemary sprig and a halved lemon slice each. Place a few slices of lemon and some rosemary on either side of each mullet and hold in place with kitchen twine. Baste the fish with a little olive oil and braise for 5 minutes under the preheated grill. Remove the twine, season with coarse sea salt and serve.

This dish matches perfectly with jacket potatoes served with herb mascarpone or baked potatoes seasoned with rosemary.

CHAMPINIONS AMB MOLL DE FANG
CHAMPIÑONES CON SALMONETES
BUTTON MUSHROOMS WITH RED MULLET AND SPINACH

Catalan cooking often matches seafood with ingredients from the hinterland, especially in the regions along the coast. These combinations are referred to as mar i muntanya — *sea and mountains.*

Serves 4 | **Preparation:** 25 minutes | **Frying and baking time:** 25 minutes

INGREDIENTS

8 large button mushrooms

100 g (3½ oz) baby English spinach

Olive oil for frying

4 tablespoons cream

Garlic chives, thinly sliced

2 garlic cloves, thinly sliced

6 red mullet fillets

Deep-fried parsley for garnish

PREPARATION

Preheat the oven to 180°C (350°F). Snap off the mushroom stems and gently clean the mushroom tops.

Briefly wilt the spinach in a saucepan with a little olive oil over low heat. Drain on paper towel and chop. Combine the spinach and cream and season with salt. Fry the garlic chives and garlic in olive oil until crisp.

Heat an ovenproof pan over medium heat. Add some olive oil and briefly sear the mushroom tops. Sprinkle the insides with a little salt and stuff with the spinach mixture. Bake the mushrooms on the middle rack of the oven until done, about 3 minutes.

Cut the red mullet fillets into even pieces about 5 x 5 cm (2 x 2 inches). Briefly sear the mullet pieces in a non-stick pan over high heat on both sides. Season with salt and freshly ground black pepper.

Assemble two pieces of fish each on the stuffed mushrooms (use toothpicks to hold them in place). Serve garnished with crispy fried parsley and the fried chives and garlic.

ESCAMARLANS AMB CREMA DE ALVOCAT

CIGALA CON CREMA DE AGUACATE
NORWAY LOBSTER WITH AVOCADO CREAM

Norway lobster must surely be among the most exquisite seafood around.
It is an essential ingredient in any seafood paella or fideua and is delicious simply served
a la plancha or barbecued. However, there are also more refined recipes such as the one
below, which I once enjoyed in the 'Etapes' restaurant.

Serves 4 | **Preparation:** 20 minutes | **Cooking time:** 10 minutes | **Chilling time:** 4–5 hours

INGREDIENTS
For the avocado cream

4 ripe avocados

2 tablespoons cream

Juice of 1 lime

4 tablespoons olive oil

1 French shallot, finely diced

For the Norway lobster

1 ripe tomato, peeled, seeded
   and finely diced

1 green capsicum (pepper),
   finely diced

1 French shallot, finely diced

4 tablespoons olive oil

1 teaspoon *pimentón de la vera*
   (semi-hot paprika)

12 Norway lobsters or scampi,
   about 150 g (5½ oz) each,
   deveined

Chervil leaves or chopped chives
   for garnish

PREPARE THE AVOCADO CREAM

Halve the avocados, remove the stones and transfer the flesh to a bowl. Combine with the cream, lime juice, olive oil and shallot and blend until smooth. Season with salt and freshly ground black pepper and freeze or transfer to an ice cream maker for 4–5 hours. Stir every 30 minutes, if possible.

FRY AND PLATE THE NORWAY LOBSTER

Dress the tomato, capsicum and shallot with the olive oil and paprika in a bowl.

Remove the heads of the Norway lobsters. Shell the tails except for the last segment on each lobster and season with salt. Sear in a non-stick pan over medium heat.

Arrange 3 Norway lobsters with a little salad and 1 ball of the iced avocado cream each on plates and serve garnished with chervil leaves or chopped chives.

TIP

If serving this dish as a starter, count only one Norway lobster per person and serve with a leafy salad, for example baby English spinach, baby beetroot and radicchio, instead of vegetables. For a very sophisticated presentation, thinly slice a zucchini (courgette) lengthwise and roll up to form a ring to hold each lobster as shown.

TELLERINES A LA PLANCHA
COQUINAS A LA PLANCHA
FRIED COCKLES

Even 15 years ago, one would find entire families digging around in the shallows along Barcelona's beaches, all searching for Mediterranean cockles for their lunch or dinner tables. These days, however, this has become a much rarer sight. Cockles a la plancha are an absolute delicacy that couldn't be easier to prepare! In the restaurants along the beach, cockles are often served under the name of tallarines, but it's best to check before ordering anything by this name, as the same word can also mean 'tagliatelle'.

Serves 4 | **Preparation:** 10 minutes | **Cooking time:** 10 minutes | **Cockle cleaning time:** 3–4 hours

INGREDIENTS

600 g (1 lb 5 oz) cockles
1 garlic clove, thily sliced
Olive oil
Juice of ½ lemon
Flat-leaf (Italian) parsley, chopped,
   for garnish

PREPARATION

If you plan to cook cockles collected from a sandy beach at home, it's best to ensure that they are given enough time to self-clean, as there's nothing more unpleasant than chewing on sand. To do this, immerse the cockles (or any type of mussels) in a bowl of salt water a few hours before you intend to start cooking. Use 50 g (1¾ oz) salt per 1 litre (35 fl oz) water and change the water two or three times.

Clean the cockles as described above, then heat a pan over very high heat and fry the cockles together with the garlic for about 3–4 minutes, covered, so that the shells open. Shake the pan and discard any cockles that have not opened. Add a generous splash of olive oil and the lemon juice. Season with freshly ground white pepper and serve on a platter, garnished with the parsley.

CLOÏSSES AMB BORRATJA

ALMEJAS CON BORRAJAS
CLAMS IN A BORAGE STOCK

Borage grows wild just about everywhere around Barcelona. Elsewhere in Europe, it is cultivated and used as a salad herb or seasoning for cucumber dishes. In the past, borage was not only used as a healing herb, but also prepared as a healthy vegetable of its own, according to a range of creative recipes, and it might just be time for us to remember these old traditions!

Serves 4 | **Preparation:** 15 minutes | **Cooking time:** 20 minutes

INGREDIENTS

300 g (10½ oz) borage

100 ml (3½ fl oz) olive oil

1 garlic clove, crushed

1 heaped tablespoon plain
   (all-purpose) flour

4 tablespoons white wine

400 g (14 oz) clams, cleaned
   (see page 154)

4–5 sprigs flat-leaf (Italian)
   parsley, chopped

PREPARATION

Wash the borage and blanch whole (stems and leaves) for about 5 minutes in lightly salted boiling water. Drain, cut into pieces and reserve the cooking liquid.

Heat a pan over low heat, add the olive oil and sauté the garlic, stirring constantly to prevent any browning. Add the flour and sweat briefly. Add the white wine and about 200 ml (7 fl oz) of the borage cooking water. Bring everything to the boil and simmer for 2 minutes. Add the clams to the sauce and continue to cook for another 2 minutes until they open, then add the borage and parsley. Season with salt and freshly ground white pepper. Continue to simmer for 2 minutes and then serve with fresh white bread.

CLOÏSSES A LA MARINERA
ALMEJAS A LA MARINERA
CLAMS IN A HEARTY SAUCE

Cloïsses a la marinera *is a delicacy that is available all year round. Virtually all restaurants, especially those directly on the beaches, have this simple, yet entirely delicious, dish on their menus. Fresh clams should be cleaned in salt water before cooking (see page 154).*

Serves 4 | **Preparation:** 10 minutes | **Cooking time:** 30 minutes

INGREDIENTS

100 ml (3½ fl oz) white wine

2 bay leaves

500 g (1 lb 2 oz) large or
   1 kg (2 lb 4 oz) small clams

50 ml (1½ fl oz) olive oil

1 onion, chopped

1 garlic clove, finely minced

1 teaspoon sweet paprika

1 tablespoon plain (all-purpose)
   flour

2 ripe tomatoes, peeled, seeded
   and finely diced

1 small dried red chilli, seeded
   and chopped

PREPARATION

Add half of the wine, a little water and the bay leaves to a large pan and heat over very high heat. Add the clams, cover and steam for 3–4 minutes until the shells open. Do this in several batches, if necessary. Remove and discard any shells that do not open. Strain the clam broth through a piece of muslin (cheesecloth) and reserve.

Heat the olive oil in a pan over medium heat. Add the onion and garlic and sauté until golden brown. Reduce the heat. Thoroughly stir in the paprika and flour to form a roux. Continue to simmer for 3–4 minutes, then add the remaining wine and reserved clam broth. Simmer to reduce the liquid. Stir in the tomatoes and dried chilli. Return the clams to the thickened sauce after about 10 minutes. Bring to the boil over high heat and stir well.

Serve with white bread.

Some shops specialise in deli products.

GAMBAS AMB ROMESCO
GAMBAS CON ROMESCO
PRAWNS IN ROMESCO SAUCE

This dish is based on a variation of the traditional romesco sauce, which imparts a unique flavour.

Serves 4 | **Preparation:** 10 minutes | **Cooking time:** 20 minutes

INGREDIENTS

100 ml (3½ fl oz) olive oil

12–16 large or king prawns (shrimp)

For the romesco sauce

1 garlic clove, thinly sliced

80 g (2¾ oz) almonds, blanched
    and peeled

1 small onion, diced

2 small red chillies, seeded
    and minced

3 large ripe tomatoes, peeled,
    seeded and finely diced

1 bay leaf

4–5 sprigs flat-leaf (Italian)
    parsley, chopped

1 slice stale white bread, diced

Sherry vinegar

PREPARE THE PRAWNS

Heat a little olive oil in a pan over high heat. Add the prawns to sear, then remove from the pan and set aside.

PREPARE THE ROMESCO SAUCE

Add the garlic and almonds to the pan together with a little olive oil. Fry over high heat until golden brown, then remove from the pan and set aside. Sauté the onion in a little more olive oil until translucent. Add the chillies, tomatoes and bay leaf. Increase the heat and simmer to reduce a little.

Meanwhile, crush the garlic, almonds, parsley and white bread in a mortar and pestle or blend with a stick blender. Add the mixture to the sauce along with a little water and season with salt, freshly ground white pepper and sherry vinegar.

Add the prawns to the hot sauce and simmer gently for a few minutes. Be careful not to allow the sauce to boil.

PAELLA AMB MARISCS

PAELLA DE MARISCOS
SEAFOOD PAELLA

Everybody knows this Spanish rice dish, but did you know that it is named after the special pan in which it is prepared? Paella originated in the region around Valencia and Alicante. In the past, it was usually cooked on Thursdays, which was the day before fish and seafood were traditionally bought fresh again from the markets. Paella recipes vary between one region and the next, and recipes differ even between different parts of Barcelona. Try to avoid eating paella on Barcelona's Ramblas – you'll find it better and cheaper in other streets that are less frequented by tourists.

Serves 4–6 | **Preparation:** 25 minutes | **Cooking and frying time:** 40 minutes

INGREDIENTS

200 ml (7 fl oz) olive oil

2 garlic cloves, thinly sliced

2 dried nyora peppers from
   specialist suppliers or 2 g (¹⁄₁₆ oz)
   saffron (see tip on page 166)

1 small glass white wine

8 large prawns (shrimp)

4 large Norway lobsters or scampi

1 onion, finely chopped

250 g (9 oz) squid, finely diced

400 g (14 oz) short-grain rice
   (*arroz bomba*)

3 tomatoes, peeled, seeded and
   finely diced

1.5 litres (52 fl oz) fish stock (see
   recipe on page 261)

1 red capsicum (pepper), roasted,
   peeled and diced

200 g (7 oz) each mussels and
   clams (vongole), cleaned
   (see page 154)

PREPARE THE VEGETABLES AND SEAFOOD

Heat a large, deep paella pan or frying pan over high heat. Add a little olive oil and fry the garlic and dried nyora peppers until golden brown. Remove the peppers from the pan and drain well on paper towel. Once cool, crush them to a fine powder in a mortar and pestle. Combine the powder with the white wine and set aside.

Heat a little olive oil in the pan over high heat. Add the prawns and Norway lobsters and sear all over, then remove from the pan and set aside.

Reduce the heat to medium and add a little more olive oil to the pan, together with the onion. Sauté until translucent, then add the diced squid and sear. Remove from the pan and set aside.

PREPARE THE RICE

Heat the remaining olive oil in the pan, add the rice and sauté over medium heat for 2 minutes. Stir in the tomatoes, 1 litre (35 fl oz) of the fish stock and the wine mixture. Stir in the capsicum and season to taste. Increase the heat to high and boil the rice in the stock for 5 minutes, then reduce the heat again and continue to cook for another 7–8 minutes. Add more fish stock if the rice turns too dry. Season again.

PUT TOGETHER THE PAELLA

Stir the clams into the rice and arrange the remaining seafood decoratively on top, with the mussels around the edge of the pan. Cover the pan and cook over medium heat until done, about 3–4 minutes. Ideally, the rice will start to stick to the pan – the crunchy rice is almost the best thing about a paella. Remove the paella from the heat and leave to rest, covered, for 5 minutes before serving.

ARRÒS DE GALERAS AMB CARXOFES

ARROZ CON GALERAS Y ACACHOFEAS
MANTIS SHRIMP AND ARTICHOKES ON RICE

Galeras or mantis shrimp are unusual-looking creatures that are not particularly well known outside Spain, and even here they are mainly used as an ingredient in stocks and soups. This doesn't do them justice, though, as mantis shrimp taste excellent, even though they have relatively little flesh and are quite tricky to shell. If you prefer, you can substitute any other saltwater prawns.

Serves 4 | **Preparation:** 10 minutes | **Cooking time:** 40 minutes

INGREDIENTS

Olive oil for frying

200 g (7 oz) artichoke hearts
(ideally fresh), thinly sliced

1 garlic clove, halved

1 small onion, finely diced

½ green capsicum (pepper),
finely diced

16 galeras (mantis shrimp) or
other large prawns (shrimp)

500 g (1 lb 2 oz) short-grain rice
(*arroz bomba*)

100 ml (3½ fl oz) white wine

100 ml (3½ fl oz) brandy

3 ripe tomatoes, peeled, seeded
and finely diced

2 dried nyora peppers from
specialist suppliers or 2 g (1/16 oz)
saffron (see tip)

1.5 litres (52 fl oz) seafood or fish
stock (see recipe on page 261)

PREPARATION

Heat a large, deep pan over high heat. Add olive oil, the artichoke hearts and garlic and fry for 5 minutes. Remove from the pan and set aside.

Add 4 tablespoons olive oil to the same pan and sweat the onion and capsicum until translucent over medium heat. Add the shrimp and rice and continue to fry for 5 minutes. Add the white wine, brandy, tomatoes and nyora peppers or saffron. Stir in the stock and season with salt. Simmer for 20 minutes over low heat, returning the artichokes and the garlic to the stock after about 10 minutes. Peel some of the shrimp before serving; fold others in with the rice. Serve garnished with the peeled shrimp.

TIP

Nyora peppers are reddish-black, plum-sized dried peppers with an aromatic, slightly bitter, mildly spicy flavour. If you can get nyora peppers, use them to impart a unique aroma and colour to just about any rice or pasta dish. To prepare, remove the stem base and seeds from 1 nyora pepper. Thinly slice 1 garlic clove. Fry both in hot olive oil until the garlic has turned golden brown, but be careful not to burn the garlic. Reserve the oil for later use and discard the garlic. Drain the pepper and leave to cool. It will have turned brittle. Finely crush the cooled pepper in a mortar and pestle together with a little coarse sea salt. Stir into fish stock; note that you may then be able to reduce other seasonings to taste.

Nyora peppers are sometimes also referred to as Nora chillies. Columbus first brought them back from the New World and left them with monks in the congregation of La Nora in Spain, hence the name.

ARRÒS NEGRE AMB SIPIA
ARROZ NEGRO CON SEPIA
BLACK RICE WITH SQUID

When I first had this dish put in front of me at a table, I had serious doubts whether I'd enjoy it. But be bold: black rice, coloured with squid ink, is a true delicacy. Squid ink is available from good fishmongers, or you can order it online. Or go to Barcelona…

Serves 4 | **Preparation:** 10 minutes | **Cooking time:** 30 minutes

INGREDIENTS

600–750 g (1 lb 5 oz–1 lb 10 oz)
    squid tubes
Olive oil for frying
1 onion, finely diced
1 small garlic clove, crushed
½ red capsicum (pepper),
    finely diced
1 large tomato, peeled, seeded
    and finely diced
1 teaspoon paprika
4 sachets squid ink, about 4 g
    (⅛ oz) each
300 g (10½ oz) short-grain rice
    (*arroz bomba*)
750 ml (26 fl oz) hot fish stock
    (see recipe on page 261)

PREPARATION

Finely dice the squid tubes. Heat a little olive oil in a large frying pan. Briefly sauté the onion and garlic over medium heat. Add the capsicum, season with salt and continue to cook for about 5 minutes, stirring constantly. Stir in the tomato and continue to simmer for a few more minutes.

Fold in the paprika, squid ink, diced squid and rice. Add the hot fish stock. Increase the heat to high and simmer for 5 minutes. Reduce the heat and simmer for another 13–15 minutes, adding more fish stock if necessary. Once the rice has cooked, remove the pan from the heat. Cover and set aside to rest for a few minutes. Serve with *all i oli* (see page 260).

FIDEOS AMB MARISCS
FIDEOS CON MARISCOS
SEAFOOD FIDEO PASTA

Anyone who believes that Italy is the only true home of pasta is entirely wrong. Catalans have been eating and enjoying pasta for over 500 years – remember that parts of modern-day Italy once belonged to the kingdom of Catalonia. The most popular pasta types are canelones *and* fideos. Fideos *are short, thin semolina vermicelli, which can be prepared in a seemingly endless variety of ways. Feel free to vary the seafood in this recipe to your preference. This is the Catalan response to Valencia's seafood paella.*

Serves 4 | **Preparation:** 10 minutes | **Frying and baking time:** 45 minutes

INGREDIENTS

150 ml (5½ fl oz) olive oil

400 g (14 oz) fideo pasta No. 1
    or another type of short,
    thin pasta

1 onion, finely diced

200 g (7 oz) squid tubes, sliced

1 litre (35 fl oz) hot fish stock
    (see recipe on page 261)

200 g (7 oz) clams, cleaned
    (see page 154)

8 mussels, cleaned

16 prawns (shrimp), peeled
    and deveined

PREPARATION

Preheat the oven to 150°C (300°F). Heat the olive oil in an ovenproof pan over medium heat and fry the pasta until golden brown. Once it starts to brown, add the onion and sweat until translucent, stirring constantly. Quickly stir in the squid and fry everything for a few more minutes. Pour in the hot fish stock and simmer over medium heat for 5 minutes, stirring constantly.

Transfer the pan to the middle rack of the oven and bake for 12–15 minutes until all of the liquid has been absorbed. Remove from the oven and add the remaining seafood. Reduce the temperature a little, cover the pan and cook until done, 5–10 minutes.

ARRÒS AMB GAMBES I FONOLL
ARROZ CON GAMBAS Y HINOJO
PRAWNS AND FENNEL ON RICE

Catalans eat many varieties of rice, but their absolute favourite is arroz bomba, *short-grain rice from the Ebro delta, which is commonly used for paella dishes. For this recipe, you can substitute any good Italian risotto rice. Fennel adds a fresh flavour to the dish. I love to use wild fennel, which grows right outside my door here in Barcelona, as it has a much richer aroma.*

Serves 4 | **Preparation:** 20 minutes | **Cooking time:** 1¼ hours

INGREDIENTS
For the *fumet* bouillabaisse
Prawn (shrimp) heads and shells,
   small prawns or other shrimp
60 g (2¼ oz) butter
1 garlic clove, thinly sliced
40 g (1½ oz) carrots, finely diced
40 g (1½ oz) onions, finely diced
¼ bulb fennel, finely diced
150 ml (5½ fl oz) white wine

For the prawns and rice
Olive oil for frying
200 g (7 oz) squid tubes, finely diced
1 onion, finely diced
500 g (1 lb 2 oz) large prawns
   (shrimp), peeled and deveined
100 g (3½ oz) risotto rice
125 ml (4 fl oz) cream
Fennel or dill fronds for garnish

COOK THE *FUMET*
For the fumet bouillabaisse, coarsely mash the prawn heads and shells with the prawns in a mortar and pestle. Heat a saucepan over medium heat. Melt the butter, add the seafood, garlic and vegetables and sauté. Add the white wine and 500 ml (17 fl oz) water. Simmer for 30 minutes, then strain and set aside.

PREPARE THE PRAWNS AND RICE
Heat a little olive oil in a frying pan over medium heat and fry the squid and onion. Set aside the best 4 prawns. Coarsely chop the other prawns and add to the pan. Fold in the rice and sauté everything. Add enough of the strained *fumet* to cover and simmer for 18–20 minutes, stirring constantly with a wooden spoon. Season with salt and freshly ground white pepper and add the cream right at the end of the cooking time.

Briefly fry the whole prawns in olive oil in another pan. Arrange the rice on plates using ring moulds and top with 1 fried prawn each. Garnish with fennel fronds or dill, carefully pour a bed of *fumet* around the rice and serve.

OSMOSIS

There is certainly no shortage of creativity among Barcelona's chefs and restaurateurs. One of my favourite restaurants, 'Osmosis', has established its own niche in the city's rich culinary scene. It only uses the freshest of ingredients and doesn't even have a store room, as everything comes straight from the market.

Once a week, chef Fredereic Fernandez and his team cook a five-course degustation menu, which is always based around a soup, a rice dish or salad, and fish, followed by poultry or meat and finally dessert. But that's not all: the menu starts off with an amuse-gueule, generally a home-made *foie micuit* (duck or goose foie gras) and finishes with a second dessert that involves chocolate three ways. It's best to leave the choice of wines to the sommelier, who happens to be the co-owner of 'Osmosis'. Here you'll find heaven on a plate!

GUATLLES AMB PEBROTS VERMELLS
CODORNICES CON PIMIENTOS ROJOS ASADOS
QUAIL AND QUAIL EGGS ON MARINATED CAPSICUM

This dish serves up quail in two distinct flavours. Escabeche *is a tasty sauce in which the quail is slowly simmered for an incomparably tender result.*

Serves 4 | **Preparation:** 25 minutes | **Cooking and frying time:** 1¾ hours

INGREDIENTS

For the quail
4 kitchen-ready quails
Soy sauce for the marinade
Olive oil for frying

For the *escabeche*
1 onion, finely diced
1 carrot, finely diced
1 garlic clove, crushed
1 bay leaf
5–6 black peppercorns,
   lightly crushed
150 ml (5 fl oz) olive oil
50 ml (1½ fl oz) sherry vinegar
50 ml (1½ fl oz) dry sherry

For the quail eggs
Vinegar
12 fresh quail eggs

For serving
Marinated grilled capsicums
   (see recipe on page 262)

PREPARE THE QUAIL AND *ESCABECHE*

Separate the quail legs, place in a bowl and cover with soy sauce. Leave to marinate while preparing the rest of the dish. Discard the necks and wings, as they are not used in this recipe.

Combine the ingredients for the *escabeche* in a saucepan and heat over medium heat. Add the quail breasts and simmer until soft, about 1½ hours. Season with salt and freshly ground black pepper. Take the quail breasts out of the saucepan and remove the skin and bones. Return the breasts to the *escabeche* to keep warm.

Heat the olive oil in a frying pan over medium heat. Remove the quail legs from the marinade and fry on all sides until done.

POACH THE QUAIL EGGS

Add salt and a dash of vinegar to a pan of water and bring to the boil. Use a wooden spoon to stir the water, creating a whirlpool. Crack the quail eggs open and slide them right into the centre of the whirlpool of boiling water, one by one. As soon as the egg whites have set, lift the poached eggs out of the water with a slotted spoon and refresh them under cold water. Remove any unsightly bits of coagulated egg white.

PLATE THE QUAILS

Remove the quail legs and breasts from the marinade and pan. Score the breasts crosswise. Divide among plates on top of warmed, marinated capsicum strips and arrange the poached eggs on the side.

TIP

For serving, combine 1 teaspoon paprika and 3 teaspoons warmed olive oil. Drizzle the finished dish with the paprika oil and a little balsamic vinegar and serve garnished with flat-leaf (Italian) parsley.

PERDIU ESCABETXADA
ESCABECHE DE PERDIZ
PARTRIDGE IN *ESCABECHE*

Escabeche *is actually a kind of acidic marinade used to preserve fish and meat. The marinated fish or meat is then generally eaten cold or just at room temperature. Partridge in* escabeche *is a very popular dish in Spain. I'm particularly fond of the following version, which is served hot in Barcelona's 'La Pitarra' restaurant. You can substitute the perdices for partridges in this recipe.*

Serves 4 | **Preparation:** 25 minutes | **Cooking and frying time:** 1 hour 50 minutes | **Marinating time:** 12 hours

INGREDIENTS

2 large, kitchen-ready partridges

1.5 litres (52 fl oz) olive oil

4 onions, finely diced

4–5 garlic cloves, crushed

2 carrots, finely diced

2 turnips, peeled and quartered

250 ml (9 fl oz) fino sherry

250 ml (9 fl oz) chicken stock

2 tablespoons black peppercorns

1 bay leaf

1 sprig thyme

BRAISE THE PARTRIDGES

Tie the partridge legs and wings to the body with kitchen twine and season the birds with salt and freshly ground black pepper. Heat a roasting pan over medium heat. Add a little olive oil and fry the birds until browned all over. Add the remaining ingredients and cook everything over low heat for at least 1½ hours.

Leave to cool, then refrigerate and marinate in the stock for 1 day.

PLATE THE PARTRIDGES

Halve the birds and carefully trim the meat off the bones. Reheat the meat in the stock. Remove from the stock and divide among plates. This goes well with *samfaina* (see page 263), *patatas al pobre* (see page 74) or mashed potatoes.

COLOMAS AMB POCHAS
PICHONES CON POCHAS
PIGEON WITH CANNELLINI BEANS

Spaniards eat a lot of poultry in general, and the local pigeons and partridges are among the finest you'll ever find in restaurants. The beans in the original recipe are Spanish pochas *beans — white beans that are harvested before they are fully ripe. You can substitute alubia beans (available from specialist suppliers) or cannellini beans, which you'll find anywhere.*

Serves 4 | **Preparation:** 25 minutes | **Frying and cooking time:** 1¼ hours

INGREDIENTS
For the poultry

4 kitchen-ready young pigeons
    or 2 partridges
40 g (1½ oz) lard
50 ml (1½ fl oz) olive oil
1 carrot, finely diced
1 small garlic clove, very
    finely crushed
5–6 sprigs flat-leaf (Italian) parsley,
    finely chopped
1 small glass brandy
150 ml (5 fl oz) meat stock

For the sauce

250 g (9 oz) young white beans
1 onion, diced
1 green capsicum (pepper), diced
3 fully ripe tomatoes, peeled,
    seeded and diced
Olive oil for frying
50 g (1¾ oz) serrano ham,
    finely diced

PREPARE THE POULTRY

Generously season the pigeons with salt. Heat the lard and olive oil in a casserole dish over medium heat. Add the pigeons, carrot, garlic and about half of the parsley and deglaze with the brandy. Cook over very low heat until the liquid has evaporated. Add the stock and continue to simmer for another 20 minutes. Add more stock if necessary.

PREPARE THE BEANS AND VEGETABLES

Meanwhile, cover the beans with water in a saucepan and simmer over medium heat until soft, about 20 minutes. Season with a little salt.

Fry the onion, capsicum and tomatoes in olive oil in a frying pan over medium heat. Cook for 20 minutes, then blend with a stick blender. Combine with the beans in the saucepan, add the diced ham and simmer everything for another 20 minutes.

Transfer the bean mixture to the casserole with the pigeons and cook until heated through. Garnish with the remaining parsley and serve in the casserole dish.

TIP

If you want to serve this dish as a starter, don't prepare it as a stew, but instead arrange the pigeons and sauce decoratively on plates, garnished with chives. Serve the beans separately and reduce the quantity of beans accordingly.

Barcelonian markets are treasure troves of exquisite ingredients and delights.

POLLASTRE FARCIT
POLLO RELLENO
STUFFED ROAST CHICKEN

This 'Sunday roast' is worth every minute of time and every cent of money necessary to get it onto the table as deliciously as possible. I therefore recommend using only the best of ingredients, above all a chicken of superior quality. It's best to have the chicken fully deboned by a butcher so you can focus on the stuffing. Ask your butcher to also remove the tips of the wings, but to leave the chicken body intact.

Serves 4 | **Preparation:** 30 minutes | **Cooking and frying time:** 1 hour 10 minutes | **Resting time:** 12 hours

INGREDIENTS

1 kitchen-ready chicken for roasting

1 fresh, lean botifarra, cut into pieces

3–4 slices edam or emmental cheese

3–4 slices bacon

1 small jar of pimientos del piquillo

2–3 hard-boiled eggs, quartered

8 olives, pitted

200 g (7 oz) fresh red pine mushrooms, cleaned, or 150 g (5½ oz) mushrooms from a jar, drained

Olive oil for frying

4–5 onions, diced

2 tablespoons almonds and hazelnuts, coarsely chopped

1 chicken or vegetable stock cube

600 ml (21 fl oz) beer

STUFF AND SEAR THE CHICKEN

Spread the chicken flat on your workbench. Season the inside with salt and freshly ground black pepper. Spread with botifarra and top with the sliced cheese, bacon, pimientos, eggs, olives and a good third of the mushrooms. Roll up like a Swiss roll and tie together firmly with kitchen twine so that the stuffing cannot fall out.

Heat some olive oil in a roasting pan over high heat and fry the onions. Add the stuffed chicken and fry on all sides. Keep loosening it from the pan to prevent it from burning.

COOK THE CHICKEN IN THE SAUCE

Add the chopped almonds and hazelnuts, the crumbled stock cube and the remaining mushrooms and deglaze with the beer. Bring to the boil over high heat, then reduce the heat and continue to simmer the chicken. The chicken is cooked when no liquid escapes from the meat when it is pierced with a wooden skewer.

Leave the chicken to cool in the stock and then allow to rest overnight. The next day, slice the cold chicken and return it to the gravy. Reheat in a hot oven and serve.

POLLASTRE AMB ESCAMARLANS

POLLO CON CIGALAS
CHICKEN WITH SEAFOOD

Catalans have a special name for dishes that combine seafood with meat, poultry or vegetables from the hinterland: mar i muntanya *— sea and mountain, and these recipes are very distinctively Catalan. Mar i muntanya food is the product of Catalan chefs' innovative and adventurous approach to their craft. Do try them — I promise you'll be rewarded with many pleasant surprises. By the way, chocolate has been used in Catalan cooking since Columbus first brought it back from the New World.*

Serves 4 | **Preparation:** 20 minutes | **Cooking and frying time:** 40 minutes

INGREDIENTS
For the chicken

1 kitchen-ready chicken, about
   1–1.5 kg (2 lb 4 oz–3 lb 5 oz)
100 ml (3½ fl oz) olive oil
1 onion, finely diced
2 ripe tomatoes, peeled, seeded
   and diced
1 bay leaf
125 ml (4 fl oz) semi-dry white wine
250 ml (9 fl oz) chicken stock

For the *picada*

10 g (¼ oz) blanched almonds
3–4 saffron threads
1 tablespoon dark chocolate, grated
1 tablespoon breadcrumbs
1 tablespoon cognac
1 tablespoon flat-leaf (Italian)
   parsley, chopped
8 large Norway lobsters, scampi
   or crayfish

PREPARATION

Divide the chicken into pieces. Season with salt and pepper. Heat a little olive oil in a casserole dish over high heat, add the chicken pieces and sear.

Add the onion and sauté until translucent, then add the tomatoes, bay leaf, white wine and stock. Bring to the boil and simmer everything for 10–15 minutes.

Combine the remaining olive oil and all of the ingredients for the *picada*, except the seafood, in a mortar and pestle and pound to a paste. Add the paste to the chicken, stir in well and return everything to the boil.

Add the Norway lobsters and simmer in the stock for 5–8 minutes. Season with salt and pepper and serve in the casserole dish.

ANEC AL FORN AMB PRUNES I PINYONS

PATO AL HORNO CON CIRUELAS Y PIÑONES
ROAST DUCK WITH PRUNES AND PINE NUTS

People in the region around Barcelona eat a lot of duck, and the nearby Penedès region produces excellent birds. Duck dishes such as this one, which is prepared with prunes, pine nuts and cinnamon, are available year round, even though the ingredients might suggest a Christmas dish.

Serves 4 | **Preparation:** 25 minutes | **Cooking time:** 1 hour 50 minutes

INGREDIENTS

1 kitchen-ready duck, about 1.5 kg
   (3 lb 5 oz)

1 tablespoon olive oil

2–3 garlic cloves, unpeeled

1 onion, diced

1 carrot, diced

1 small leek, sliced

1 bay leaf

1 sprig thyme

1 cinnamon stick

100 ml (3½ fl oz) white wine

100 ml (3½ fl oz) cognac

2 tomatoes, peeled, seeded
   and diced

12 prunes, pitted

40 g (1½ oz) pine nuts

PREPARATION

Preheat the oven to 160°C (320°F). Season the duck with salt and freshly ground black pepper. Heat the olive oil and garlic in a roasting pan over high heat and brown the duck all over. Add the onion, carrot, leek, bay leaf, thyme and cinnamon stick. Deglaze with a little water. Cook on the middle rack of the preheated oven, basting occasionally with the meat juices and adding a little more water as required.

After 1 hour, add first the wine, then the cognac and reduce the liquid before adding the diced tomatoes. Cook for another 30 minutes, then remove the duck and vegetables from the pan. Remove the garlic and discard. Pass the vegetables and gravy through a sieve. Return to the roasting dish together with the prunes and pine nuts. Quarter the duck and also return to the pan. Continue to cook for another 10 minutes. Arrange decoratively on a large platter and serve with deep-fried potatoes.

CARGOLS AMB SOBRASSADA

CARACOLES CON SOBRASSADA
SNAILS WITH SOBRASSADA SAUSAGE

This method for cooking snails originally comes from Mallorca.
For the recipe below, the snails are pre-cooked.

Serves 4 | **Preparation:** 15 minutes | **Cooking time:** 1 hour 20 minutes

INGREDIENTS

1 kg (2 lb 4 oz) banded snails

1 bay leaf

2–3 sprigs rosemary

5–6 fennel fronds

Olive oil for frying

1 onion, diced

4 large ripe tomatoes, peeled,
   seeded and diced

3–4 slices serrano ham, thinly sliced

100 g (3½ oz) sobrassada
   (Mallorcan spreadable sausage)
   in small pieces

1 garlic clove, crushed

1–2 small dried chillies (*guindillas*),
   crumbled

3–4 sprigs flat-leaf (Italian)
   parsley, chopped

1 small red capsicum (pepper),
   roasted, peeled and diced

200 ml (7 fl oz) white wine

1 tablespoon dark chocolate, grated

PREPARATION

Clean the snails under running water and transfer them to a large pot. Add the bay leaf, rosemary and fennel and pour in enough water to cover. Bring to the boil over medium heat and boil for about 1 hour.

Meanwhile, heat the olive oil in a casserole dish and sauté the onion until translucent. Add the tomatoes and ham and season with salt and freshly ground black pepper. Once the tomatoes have softened, stir in the sobrassada until well combined.

Combine the garlic, chilli and parsley to a paste in a mortar and pestle. Dilute the paste with a little cooking water from the snails and add to the tomato mixture. Stir in the capsicum. Add the snails, wine and chocolate and continue to simmer everything for about 20 minutes. Serve with white bread.

LLOM DE CERDO AMB FIGUES
SOLOMILLO DE CERDO CON HIGOS
PORK LOIN WITH FIGS

In the past, most people in Spain, like most people anywhere, could only afford to have meat dishes on special occasions. Pork loin with figs and Pedro Jiménez sauce is a simple, yet sophisticated, meat dish.

Serves 4 | **Preparation:** 15 minutes | **Cooking, frying and roasting time:** 55 minutes

INGREDIENTS

For the side

1 tablespoon raisins

8 dried figs or pitted prunes, halved

Sherry for marinating

For the pork loin

1 kg (2 lb 4 oz) pork loin

Olive oil for frying

125 ml (4 fl oz) sweet sherry (e.g. Pedro Jiménez)

1 large onion, quartered and thinly sliced

1 tablespoon plain (all-purpose) flour

150–200 ml (5–7 fl oz) hot chicken stock

Sea salt flakes

3–4 small sprigs thyme

PREPARE THE SIDE DISH

Soak the raisins and dried figs or prunes in the sherry and set aside.

ROAST THE PORK LOIN

Preheat the oven to 150°C (300°F). Trim any skin, tendons or fat off the pork loin. Trim off the ends and use elsewhere. Cut the meat into four even pieces. Heat the olive oil in an ovenproof pan over high heat and sear the pork loin all over. Cover, transfer to the middle rack of the oven and roast until cooked through, about 15–20 minutes.

PREPARE THE SAUCE

Deglaze the meat juices in the roasting pan with the sherry. Heat some more olive oil in another pan over medium heat and caramelise the onion with a little salt. Once the onion is lightly caramelised, stir in the flour and cook for another minute before adding the sherry stock. Bring everything to the boil. Add the soaked dried fruit and simmer to reduce somewhat. Pour in the chicken stock and simmer for about 15 minutes to make a creamy gravy. Season with salt and freshly ground black pepper.

PUT THE DISH TOGETHER

Season the pork loin with pepper and arrange the slices on warmed plates. Pour the gravy around the meat slices and divide the dried fruit among the plates. Garnish with sea salt flakes and sprigs of thyme. Serve with potatoes.

PEUS DE PORC AMB BOLETS
PIES DE CERDO CON SETAS
MUSHROOM-STUFFED PIG'S TROTTERS

Once upon a time, literally every single bit of a butchered pig was used in one way or another. Nothing was thrown away, and even the bristles, snout and all offal were put to some use, as were the trotters, which are surprisingly delicious. Catalans have a range of recipes for this somewhat undervalued piece of pork.

Serves 8 | **Preparation:** 40 minutes | **Cooking time:** 2 hours 10 minutes

INGREDIENTS
For the pig's trotters

8 pig's trotters (available from butchers)

1 onion, chopped

1 bay leaf

1 clove

5 black peppercorns

1 bunch of soup vegetables, cut into large pieces

Olive oil for frying

For the sauce and filling

Olive oil for frying

1 onion, diced

150 ml (5 fl oz) cava

2 tomatoes, peeled, seeded and diced

1 kg (2 lb 4 oz) wild mushrooms, cleaned and diced

1 tablespoon plain (all-purpose) flour

12 blanched almonds, chopped

12 hazelnuts, chopped

1 tablespoon flat-leaf (Italian) parsley leaves

1 garlic clove

COOK THE PIG'S TROTTERS

Thoroughly wash the pig's trotters. Bring to the boil in a pot with plenty of water, together with the onion, bay leaf, clove, peppercorns, soup vegetables and some salt. Simmer for 1½–2 hours. Remove the meat from the stock, leave to cool and carefully remove the bones. Season the meat and sear in a pan with a little added olive oil. Set aside. Strain the stock and reserve.

PREPARE THE SAUCE AND FILLING

Heat some olive oil in a saucepan over low heat and sauté the diced onion. Once the onion starts to colour, gradually deglaze with the cava. Simmer to reduce the liquid and soften the onion. Add the tomatoes and simmer until soft. Season the sauce with salt.

Dust the mushrooms with a little flour. Heat some olive oil in a pan over high heat and sear the mushrooms. Stuff the pig's trotters with the mushrooms, transfer to the pan and drizzle with the sauce. Add a little of the reserved strained stock and simmer everything for 10 minutes over low heat.

Thoroughly pound the nuts, parsley and garlic in a mortar and pestle and sprinkle over the dish. Simmer for another 10 minutes, season with salt and pepper and serve.

SECRETO IBÉRICO
SECRETO IBÉRICO
'HIDDEN' FILLET

Secreto ibérico or presa ibérica *is a delicacy that may not be very readily available, but is invariably greeted with great enthusiasm whenever it is. This cut of pork is a fan-shaped muscle located between a pig's saddle and loin. Depending on how the pork is cut, this section of loin is often hardly discernible between the layers of fat, hence the name 'hidden' fillet. It is richly marbled with fat, giving it its unique flavour.*

Serves 4 | **Preparation:** 10 minutes | **Resting time:** 12 hours | **Cooking time:** 10 minutes

INGREDIENTS

4 *secretos* or 2 fan-shaped
    secreto pieces
A little olive oil
Herbs to taste, e.g. rosemary
    or thyme
1 garlic clove, thinly sliced
Sea salt flakes

PREPARATION

Marinate the *secreto ibérico* overnight in the olive oil, herbs and garlic.

Grill (broil) the marinated meat over high heat until medium done. Slice into fine strips. Sprinkle with sea salt flakes and enjoy. This matches perfectly with *pimientos de padrón* (see page 34) or any other fried vegetables or deep-fried potatoes.

TIP

The best *secreto* fillets come from year-old, pure-bred Iberian pigs that are kept half wild on dehesa agro-forestry land and fed on *belloras* (acorns) for three months.

CONILL AMB CARGOLS O NÍSCALOS
CONEJO CON CARACOLES O ROVELLONES
RABBIT WITH SNAILS OR RED PINE MUSHROOMS

*Catalan mushroom dishes, which are often cooked according to old family recipes,
are as varied as they are tasty. The recipe below combines mushrooms with rabbit,
cooked in a rich sauce, to create an incredibly aromatic delight.*

Serves 4 | **Preparation:** 35 minutes | **Cooking and frying time:** 1¼ hours

INGREDIENTS

1 rabbit, divided into pieces

1 tablespoon plain (all-purpose)
    flour

Olive oil for frying

1 carrot, diced

1 large onion, diced

1 green capsicum (pepper), diced

1 small ripe tomato, peeled, seeded
    and diced

2 garlic cloves, unpeeled

125 ml (4 fl oz) red wine

1 teaspoon dried marjoram

1 tablespoon basil, chopped

1 tablespoon flat-leaf (Italian)
    parsley, chopped

1 rabbit liver

4 hazelnuts

4 almonds

500 g (1 lb 2 oz) snails

Vinegar

Mixed fresh herbs

PREPARATION

Season the rabbit meat with salt and freshly ground black pepper and dust with flour. Sear all over in olive oil in a large casserole dish over high heat. Add the carrot, onion, capsicum, tomato and garlic. Braise everything for about 30–40 minutes, turning the meat occasionally. Once the rabbit is golden brown all over, deglaze with the red wine. Add water, little by little, if the pan dries out. Sprinkle with the herbs.

Heat a little olive oil in a small frying pan over medium heat and fry the rabbit liver for 5 minutes. Crush the liver together with the hazelnuts and almonds in a mortar and pestle and stir the resulting paste in with the rabbit in the casserole dish. Continue to braise for 5–10 minutes until the meat is cooked through and tender. Remove the rabbit from the sauce and keep warm. Remove the garlic cloves. Blend the sauce with a stick blender and pass through a sieve. Return the sauce to the casserole dish.

Wash the snails in water with some added salt and vinegar, then rinse them well under running water. Transfer the snails and mixed herbs to a pot of cold water. Heat slowly and simmer for about 30 minutes. Drain and add to the rabbit in the casserole dish. Briefly return everything to the boil and serve.

This is absolutely delicious with simple boiled potatoes.

TIP

Alternatively, heat some olive oil in a frying pan over high heat and sear red pine mushrooms briefly. Season with salt and pepper and add to the sauce together with all of the mushroom juices. Simmer in the sauce for about 10 minutes over medium heat until cooked through. Transfer the rabbit onto a warmed platter, drizzle with the sauce and arrange the mushrooms around the rabbit. Serve immediately.

CIVET DE SENGLAR
CIVET DE JABALÍ
BRAISED WILD BOAR

In autumn and winter, many restaurants in Barcelona serve a whole range of so-called
civet dishes. This way of preparing meat goes back to the Middle Ages: it involves marinating
the meat in wine, blood and lots of onions for at least 24 hours before it is braised.
The picada is a particularly important part of this recipe.

Serves 6 | **Preparation:** 30 minutes | **Frying and cooking time:** 2 hours 40 minutes | **Marinating time:** 2 days

INGREDIENTS
For the meat and gravy

1.5 kg (3 lb 5 oz) wild boar meat

1–2 bottles red wine

2 large onions, coarsely chopped

2 carrots, coarsely chopped

1 stick celery with leaves

1 garlic clove, thinly sliced

2 bay leaves

1 clove

2 sprigs thyme

12 black peppercorns

Olive oil for frying

150 g (5½ oz) bacon, diced

2 tablespoons plain (all-purpose)
    flour

1 small glass cognac

Meat stock

For the *picada*

1 slice stale baguette

4–5 sprigs flat-leaf (Italian) parsley

1 small garlic clove, finely diced

5 almonds, chopped

5 hazelnuts, chopped

1 tablespoon pine nuts

1 tablespoon grated dark chocolate

PREPARE AND BRAISE THE MEAT

Dice the meat and season with salt and pepper. Pour the red wine over the meat, vegetables, garlic and spices in a large bowl, ensuring that everything is well covered. Cover the bowl and set aside to marinate in a cool place for 24–48 hours. Stir and turn occasionally. Remove the meat and vegetables from the marinade, drain and set aside. Bring the marinade to the boil over high heat and reduce to a quarter of its volume.

Heat a large saucepan over medium heat, add the olive oil and fry the bacon until golden brown. Remove from the saucepan and set aside.

Dust the meat with flour and sear in olive oil over high heat. Deglaze with the cognac. Dice the onion and carrots from the marinade, add to the meat in the pan and continue to fry. Pass the marinade through a sieve and add to the meat. If necessary, add some extra stock to cover the meat.

Use kitchen twine to tie the bay leaves and thyme sprigs from the marinade to a bouquet together with the celery leaves. Add to the meat along with the fried bacon. Simmer over low heat, stirring occasionally, for 2–2½ hours. Remove the herb bouquet after 2 hours.

PREPARE THE *PICADA*

For the *picada*, dice the baguette and chop the parsley. Pound all ingredients together in a mortar and pestle, then combine with a little of the gravy. Add to the gravy about 10 minutes before the end of the cooking time. Serve in a warmed bowl. This matches perfectly with mashed potatoes or any other type of vegetables.

ARRÒS AMB CONILL
ARROZ CON CONEJO
RABBIT ON RICE

Catalans love eating rabbit, and the best rabbit dishes are made with wild rabbits, of course. Many restaurants in the countryside cook the rice for this dish with banded snails for extra flavour and richness; this also makes a very popular, typically Catalan dish.

Serves 4 | **Preparation:** 30 minutes | **Frying and cooking time:** 1 hour

INGREDIENTS

1 rabbit, from a butcher

100 ml (3½ fl oz) olive oil

1 onion, finely diced

3 large ripe tomatoes, peeled, seeded and diced

1 garlic clove, unpeeled

1 green capsicum (pepper), finely diced

2 artichoke hearts, from a jar

200 g (7 oz) fresh or frozen peas

300 g (10½ oz) short-grain rice

4–5 sprigs flat-leaf (Italian) parsley, leaves picked

4–6 saffron threads

PREPARATION

Divide the rabbit and cut the meat into cubes about 2 cm (¾ inch) in size. Heat about half of the olive oil in a casserole dish over high heat. Add the rabbit pieces and sear all over. Season with salt and freshly ground black pepper and remove from the dish. Add the onion, tomatoes, garlic clove and capsicum to the same dish, together with some extra oil if necessary. Sauté over medium heat and reduce a little. Return the rabbit to the dish and deglaze with 1 litre (35 fl oz) water. Simmer for about 20 minutes. Add the artichoke hearts, peas and rice. Continue to cook for another 20 minutes, adding more water as needed.

Meanwhile, pound the parsley leaves and saffron threads with the remaining olive oil. Stir the mixture into the meat and rice 5 minutes before they have finished cooking and season once more with salt and pepper.

ESCUDELLA I CARN D'OLLA

ESCUDELLA I CARN D'OLLA
CATALAN MEAT STEW

To me, escudella *is the most Catalan and most complex stew that I know. Most people only ever cook it for Christmas because of the number of ingredients and the considerable effort required to prepare it. Getting a good* escudella *in a basic restaurant is next to impossible, but a few good restaurants offer this stew instead of a full three-course menu during the Christmas season. My friend Marc Robles i Montes has found an easier way to prepare* escudella, *though: he had his grandmother sew a number of cotton drawstring bags, which he fills with the various ingredients for the stew and cooks all at once in a large pot. He then only needs to remove the ingredients from the bags to be able to serve them separately. True Catalan ingenuity!*

Serves 6 – 8 | **Preparation:** 25 minutes | **Cooking time:** 2 hours 40 minutes | **Soaking time:** 12 hours

INGREDIENTS
For the *pilotas*

300 g (10½ oz) mixed minced (ground) meat

1 garlic clove, crushed

3–4 sprigs flat-leaf (Italian) parsley, finely chopped

150 g (5½ oz) air-dried meat, finely chopped

1 egg

1 small stale bread roll, soaked in milk and excess milk squeezed out

1 pinch ground cinnamon

Continued on the next page

PREPARE THE *PILOTA* MIXTURE

Mix the minced meat, garlic, parsley, air-dried meat, egg and soaked bread roll until well combined. Season with salt, freshly ground black pepper and cinnamon and refrigerate.

COOK THE *ESCUDELLA*

Place all of the meat and the bones in a very large pot together with 5 litres (175 fl oz) water and the legumes. Bring to the boil. Add salt, cover and simmer for about 1 hour over medium heat. Skim off any foam regularly. Meanwhile, wash, trim and coarsely chop the vegetables. Quarter the cabbage. Add everything to the pot with the meat, except for the potatoes and cabbage. Cover again and continue to cook for another 45 minutes.

Shape the *pilota* into a loaf. Add to the pot together with the potatoes and simmer everything for another 20 minutes. Add the cabbage and simmer for 10 more minutes. Finally add the sausages and simmer gently for a final 5 minutes. Season with salt.

PUT THE STEW TOGETHER

Remove some stock from the pot and use it to cook the pasta until al dente. Keep the meat and vegetables warm in the remaining stock. Slice the meat and *pilota* and serve on a warmed platter together with the sausages, vegetables and legumes.

For the *escudella*

500 g (1 lb 2 oz) beef
200 g (7 oz) pig's snout and/or
    pig's ears (from a butcher)
½ pig's trotter
1 large veal bone (from a butcher)
½ kitchen-ready chicken
100 g (3½ oz) air-dried meat
200 g (7 oz) dried cannellini beans,
    soaked overnight
200 g (7 oz) dried chickpeas,
    soaked overnight
2 carrots
1 small turnip
½ leek
1 onion
1 stick celery
1 parsnip
8 waxy potatoes
1 small white cabbage
1 each butifarra blanca and negra
    (not blood pudding!), skins
    pricked

250 g (9 oz) *gallets*
    (large pasta shells)

CANELONS D'ESTIL CATALÀ
CANELONES AL ESTILO CATALÁN
CATALAN CANNELLONI

The first written record of canelones *apparently goes back to 1815, and they have been a staple of Catalan cooking since then. Cannelloni has been among the traditional dishes to be served at Catalan Christmas dinners for generations.*

Serves 6 | **Preparation:** 35 minutes | **Frying, cooking and baking time:** 50 minutes

INGREDIENTS
For the filling

Olive oil for frying

1 skinless chicken breast fillet, diced

200 g (7 oz) chicken liver, diced

500 g (1 lb 2 oz) lean mixed minced (ground) meat

1 large onion, diced

1 small leek, sliced

1 garlic clove, crushed

1 bay leaf

3 ripe tomatoes, peeled, seeded and diced

100 ml (3½ fl oz) dessert wine

2 tablespoons breadcrumbs

Continued on the next page

PREPARE THE FILLING

Heat some olive oil in a large, deep frying pan over high heat and fry the chicken fillet, liver, minced meat, onion, leek, garlic and bay leaf until everything starts to colour. Add the diced tomatoes and reduce the liquid. Add the wine, cover and simmer everything for 15 minutes over low heat.

Remove the pan from the heat and stir in the breadcrumbs if the mixture seems too thin. Season with salt and freshly ground black pepper.

PREPARE THE *CANELONES*

Pre-cook the pasta sheets in boiling water with a dash of olive oil according to the packet instructions. Refresh under cold water and lay the sheets out on a clean tea towel.

PREPARE THE BÉCHAMEL SAUCE

Melt the butter in a saucepan over medium heat. Stir in the flour and sweat. Add the stock and milk, stirring constantly, and bring everything to the boil. Reduce the heat and simmer for 10 minutes. Season with thyme, parsley, nutmeg, salt and pepper.

PUT TOGETHER THE *CANELONES*

Preheat the oven to 180°C (350°F). Place 1½ tablespoons of the filling on each pasta sheet. Roll up the sheets around the filling and transfer them to a greased ovenproof dish. Cover with the béchamel sauce and sprinkle with cheese. Dot with shaved butter and bake on the middle rack of the oven for about 15 minutes or until golden on top.

**For the *canelones* and
the béchamel sauce**

24 pasta sheets

Olive oil for cooking

50 g (1¾ oz) butter, plus
   some extra shavings

60 g (2¼ oz) plain
   (all-purpose) flour

500 ml (17 fl oz) chicken stock

500 ml (17 fl oz) milk

1 pinch ground thyme

1 teaspoon dried parsley

1 pinch freshly grated nutmeg

100 g (3½ oz) grated cheese
   (e.g. emmental)

The view from the Basílica de Santa Maria del Mar onto the narrow lanes of the Born/La Ribera quarter.

Oh, and Barcelona's to-die-for desserts... Most Catalan desserts are incredibly sweet and immensely rich. For some, they are heaven on a plate, while others think of them more as instruments of culinary torture.

Most of these recipes would be a long way outside any dietary guidelines, but they also include some that are not quite as rich and will delight people like me, who aren't too fond of overly sweet foods.

DESSERTS

CREMA CATALANA

CREMA CATALANA
CREMA CATALANA

One of the best-known Spanish temptations must surely be crema catalana, *a dessert that has been prepared mainly (but by no means only) for San José's Day on 19 March for centuries. It is also known under the name of crème brûlée, because a certain Frenchman casually forgot to mention where he had first enjoyed this dessert when he included it in his cookbook about a century ago. Originally, the delightfully crunchy layer on top was caramelised with a specially made iron, heated to red-hot over an open fire and then passed over the sugary cream. An easier way is to use the oven grill (broiler) or, even quicker, a small kitchen blowtorch.*

Serves 4 | **Preparation:** 10 minutes | **Cooking time:** 10 minutes | **Chilling time:** 5 hours

INGREDIENTS

200 g (7 oz) sugar

4 egg yolks

1 tablespoon cornflour (cornstarch)

Grated zest of ½ organic lemon or
   orange

1 cinnamon stick

500 ml (17 fl oz) milk

PREPARATION

Place 150 g (5½ oz) of the sugar and the egg yolks in a saucepan and whisk until foamy. Add the cornflour, lemon zest and cinnamon stick and stir in the milk. Gradually heat the mixture over medium heat, stirring constantly, until the cream begins to set.

Remove the cinnamon stick and divide the cream among four heatproof ramekins. Leave to cool and then refrigerate for 4–5 hours. Before serving, sprinkle the remaining sugar on top of the cream and melt it until golden brown, using a kitchen blowtorch or oven grill (broiler). Serve immediately.

In Barcelona, *crema catalana* is often served with filleted orange segments.

FLAN

FLAN DE HUEVOS
EGG CUSTARD

Flan would be one of the best-known and most popular desserts
in all of Spain, both in restaurants and in home cooking.

Serves 6 | **Preparation:** 15 minutes | **Cooking time:** 50 minutes
Resting time: 30 minutes | **Chilling time:** 4 hours

INGREDIENTS

300 g (10½ oz) sugar
1 teaspoon lemon juice
500 ml (17 fl oz) milk
1 vanilla pod
4 large eggs
2 egg yolks

PREPARATION

Add 150 g (5½ oz) of the sugar and 4 tablespoons water to a saucepan together with the lemon juice and caramelise until golden brown, but be careful not to burn the mixture. Divide the caramel among six flan moulds (about 1 tablespoon in each one). Gently shake the moulds to distribute the caramel evenly.

Slowly heat the milk in another saucepan over medium heat. Scrape the seeds out of the vanilla pod and add both the seeds and pod to the milk. Take the mixture off the heat just before it starts to boil. Cover and leave to rest for 30 minutes.

Preheat the oven to 160°C (320°F); do not use the fan-forced setting. Combine the eggs, egg yolks and remaining 150 g (5½ oz) of the sugar in a bowl and whisk until lightly foamy. Stir in the cooled milk mixture, discarding the vanilla pod. Carefully pour the cream into the moulds. Place the moulds inside a larger baking dish and pour enough hot water into the dish to come up halfway. Bake until set, about 40 minutes. Remove from the oven as soon as the cream has set. Leave to cool to room temperature. Cover the moulds with plastic wrap and refrigerate for at least 4 hours before serving.

To serve, carefully separate the flans from the moulds using a sharp knife and invert onto small plates.

MEL I MATÓ

MEL I MATÓ
CREAM CHEESE WITH HONEY

Mató is a delicate, unsalted yet mildly savoury goat's cream cheese from the Catalan Pyrenées. It is used to make the classic Spanish dessert mel i mató, *that is, cream cheese with honey. Because* mató *is not very readily available in Australia, I have provided a recipe with slightly modified ingredients below.*

Serves 4 | **Preparation:** 10 minutes | **Cooking time:** 10 minutes | **Chilling time:** 6 hours

INGREDIENTS

2 litres (70 fl oz) milk

Zest of 1 organic lemon, peeled off in a single, broad strip

20 g (¾ oz) rennet (available from specialist suppliers) or vinegar

Honey

Walnut kernels

Pine nuts or fresh seasonal fruit

PREPARATION

Place the milk in a saucepan together with the lemon zest and simmer for 10 minutes, then leave to cool to 70°C (160°F). Dissolve the rennet in a little water and gradually add 4 tablespoons of this mixture (or the vinegar) to the milk until it coagulates. Remove the lemon zest and leave the mixture to cool for 4–5 hours.

Drain any liquid whey, if desired, or leave it in with the cream cheese, depending on the preferred consistency. Transfer the cream cheese to a sieve and leave it to drain well, then divide it among four small moulds and refrigerate until the cheese has set and firmed up.

To serve, invert the moulds onto plates, drizzle with honey and garnish with the walnuts, pine nuts and/or fresh fruit.

TORRADETES DE SANTA TERESA
TORRIJAS CON VINO
DRUNKEN FRENCH TOASTS

*This traditional dessert is quite similar to French toast. In Barcelona,
it is mainly served during* semana santa, *the Holy Week before Easter.*

Serves 4 | **Preparation:** 15 minutes | **Cooking and frying time:** 25 minutes

INGREDIENTS

1 litre (35 fl oz) milk

1 vanilla pod

2 cinnamon sticks

250 g (9 oz) sugar

Zest of ½ organic lemon,
    peeled off in a single strip

100 ml (3½ fl oz) wine, plus some
    extra for drizzling

3 eggs

Olive oil for frying

1 small loaf of stale white bread,
    thickly sliced

Cinnamon sugar

PREPARATION

Place the milk into a saucepan. Scrape the seeds out of the vanilla pod and add both the seeds and pod to the milk along with the cinnamon sticks, sugar and lemon zest. Bring to the boil. Take the saucepan off the heat and leave to cool to room temperature. Strain the mixture into a bowl. Stir in the wine. Whisk the eggs until foamy in a separate bowl.

Heat the olive oil in a large pan over medium heat. Dip the bread slices into the milk mixture and drag them through the whisked eggs. Transfer to the pan and fry them in the olive oil for 2–3 minutes each side. Remove from the pan, drain excess oil on paper towel and sprinkle with cinnamon sugar. Drizzle with a little wine just before serving.

POMA AL FORN
MANZANA ASADA EN HOJALDRE
BAKED APPLES IN PUFF PASTRY

*Baked apples have been widely enjoyed in Spain for ages. These baked apples
in puff pastry with blackcurrant sauce are a popular dessert for autumn and winter.
They are very easy to prepare and taste amazing.*

Serves 4 | **Preparation:** 20 minutes | **Cooking and baking time:** 20 minutes

INGREDIENTS
For the apples

30 g (1 oz) butter, softened

60 g (2¼ oz) sugar, plus some
    extra for the pastry

80 g (2¾ oz) blanched almonds,
    chopped

1 tablespoon raisins

½ teaspoon ground cinnamon

4 apples

400 g (14 oz) puff pastry

For the blackcurrant sauce

30 g (1 oz) sugar

3 tablespoons blackcurrant jam

1 tablespoon cornflour (cornstarch)

1 teaspoon lemon juice

1 tablespoon blackcurrants

BAKE THE APPLES

Preheat the oven to 180°C (350°F). Combine the butter, sugar, almonds, raisins and
cinnamon in a bowl. Peel the apples and remove the cores. Fill them with the nut and
raisin mixture.

Roll out the puff pastry and cut it into strips about 2 cm (¾ inch) wide. Pour the
sugar into a flat dish and roll the apples in it. Wrap the apples with slightly overlapping
strips of puff pastry, starting from the bottom and leaving a gap at the top. Transfer the
apples to an ovenproof dish and bake them on the middle rack of the oven for about
20 minutes until the puff pastry has turned golden brown.

PREPARE THE BLACKCURRANT SAUCE

Meanwhile, put the sugar and jam in a saucepan together with 100 ml (3½ fl oz) water.
Heat slowly, stirring, over medium heat. Dissolve the cornflour in 50 ml (1½ fl oz) cold
water and add to the jam mixture once it has come to the boil. Reduce the temperature
and simmer for 5 more minutes. Stir in the lemon juice. Add the blackcurrants to the
sauce and heat through for 2 minutes.

Serve the hot baked apples together with the sauce.

PANELLETS

PANELLETS
MARZIPAN CONFECTIONERY

In Catalan-speaking regions, this sweet is traditionally made for All Saint's Day on 1 November. As rich as it is, it would also make a truly indulgent Christmas treat.

Makes about 25 large or 40–50 small balls | **Preparation:** 30 minutes
Resting time: 3 hours | **Baking time:** 10 minutes

INGREDIENTS

250 g (9 oz) sugar

Grated zest of 1 organic lemon

250 g (9 oz) ground almonds

125 g (4½ oz) potatoes, boiled
    and peeled

1 egg

70 g (2½ oz) desiccated coconut

70 g (2½ oz) pine nuts

50 g (1¾ oz) whole, blanched
    almonds

PREPARATION

Combine the sugar, lemon zest and ground almonds in a bowl. Mash the potatoes with a fork. Separate the egg and set the egg white aside. Combine the potatoes with three-quarters of the egg yolk and set the remaining egg yolk aside. Add the potatoes to the sugar mixture. Use an electric mixer or food processor to form a dough, mixing for at least 1 minute. If the dough is still too soft, add some more ground almonds; if it is too dry, add the remaining egg yolk. Refrigerate for 2–3 hours.

Combine half the dough with 50 g (1¾ oz) desiccated coconut. Roll out on baking paper, cut into pieces about 3 cm (1¼ inches) square and shape these into balls. Roll the coconut *panellets* in the left-over coconut and place them on a baking tray lined with baking paper.

Prepare the remaining half of the dough following the same method, but using pine nuts. Brush the balls with egg white, roll them in the remaining pine nuts and place them on the baking tray. Press whole almonds on top of the *panellets*.

Preheat the oven grill (broiler) to 130°C (250°F). Bake the *panellets* on the middle rack of the oven until lightly browned, about 10 minutes.

Panellets, like all marzipan confectionery, dry out quickly and should therefore be stored in an airtight container and consumed soon after baking.

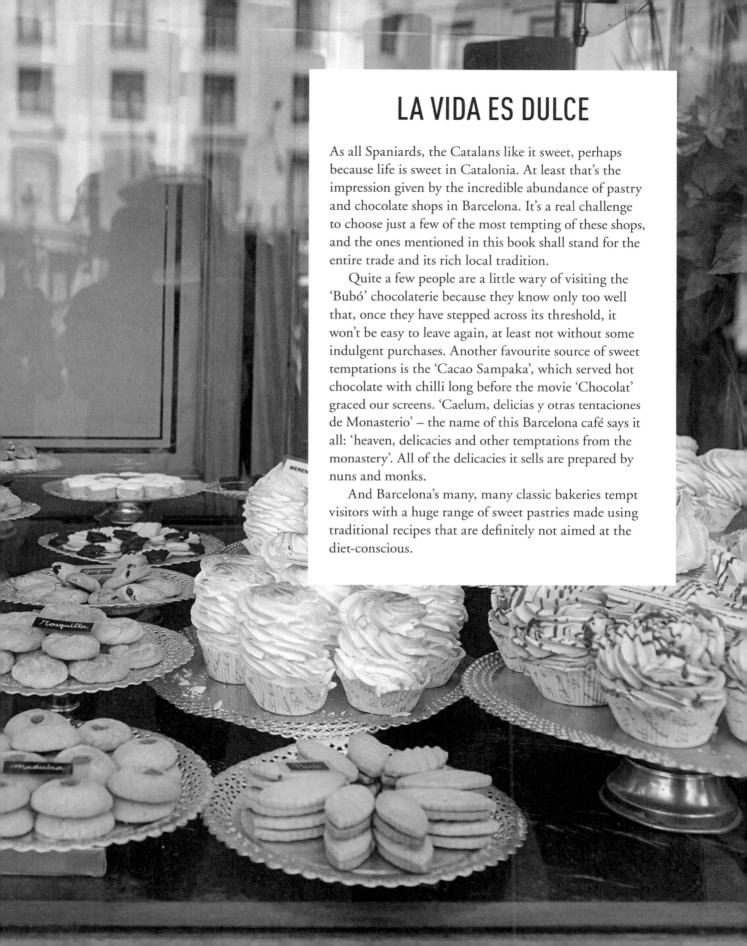

LA VIDA ES DULCE

As all Spaniards, the Catalans like it sweet, perhaps because life is sweet in Catalonia. At least that's the impression given by the incredible abundance of pastry and chocolate shops in Barcelona. It's a real challenge to choose just a few of the most tempting of these shops, and the ones mentioned in this book shall stand for the entire trade and its rich local tradition.

Quite a few people are a little wary of visiting the 'Bubó' chocolaterie because they know only too well that, once they have stepped across its threshold, it won't be easy to leave again, at least not without some indulgent purchases. Another favourite source of sweet temptations is the 'Cacao Sampaka', which served hot chocolate with chilli long before the movie 'Chocolat' graced our screens. 'Caelum, delicias y otras tentaciones de Monasterio' – the name of this Barcelona café says it all: 'heaven, delicacies and other temptations from the monastery'. All of the delicacies it sells are prepared by nuns and monks.

And Barcelona's many, many classic bakeries tempt visitors with a huge range of sweet pastries made using traditional recipes that are definitely not aimed at the diet-conscious.

COCA DE SANT JOAN

COCA DE SAN JUAN
ST JOHN'S CAKE

Coca de Sant Joan *is one of the most popular cakes in Barcelona and its surroundings. Traditionally, it is served on the eve of St John's Day, on the night from 23 to 24 June. There are thousands of variations – with or without candied fruit, with a cream made of egg yolks, sugar, milk and vanilla, with sugar and pine nuts, even with diced bacon... Decide for yourself which you like best.*

Makes 1 cake | **Preparation:** 20 minutes | **Rising time:** 45 minutes | **Baking time:** 20 minutes

INGREDIENTS
For the St John's cake

25 g (1 oz) yeast

100 ml (3½ fl oz) lukewarm milk

250 g (9 oz) plain (all-purpose) flour

100 g (3½ oz) sugar

100 g (3½ oz) butter

2 eggs

1 pinch salt

½ teaspoon ground aniseed

½ teaspoon ground cinnamon

Grated zest of ½ an organic lemon

Oil or butter for the baking tray

For the garnish

1 egg, whisked

Candied fruit

Pine nuts

Sugar

PREPARATION

Dissolve the yeast in the milk in a small bowl. Stir in 3 tablespoons of the flour to make a starter. Cover and leave the mixture to rest in a warm place for about 15 minutes.

Once the yeast mixture has doubled in volume, add the remaining ingredients and work them together to form a smooth dough. Cover again and leave to rest in a warm place for about 15 minutes until the volume has doubled again.

Shape the mixture into an oval about 1 cm (½ inch) thick and transfer to a greased baking tray. Brush with the whisked egg and decorate with the candied fruits. Leave to rest again for about 15 minutes until the volume has doubled once more. Meanwhile, preheat the oven to 160°C (320°F). Sprinkle the cake with pine nuts and sugar and bake on the middle rack of the oven for 20 minutes.

BRAÇ DE GITANO CON CREMA QUEMADA

BRAZO DE GITANO CON CREMA QUEMADA
GYPSY'S ARM CAKE

In Barcelona, when you invite guests to your home for dinner, they often bring dessert, and one of the most popular sweets to bring along is brazo de gitano. *In Australia, where we have become very politically correct, this pastry would have long been removed from any official record, as its name literally means 'gypsy's arm'.*

Makes 1 cake | **Preparation:** 35 minutes | **Cooking and baking time:** 25 minutes

INGREDIENTS

For the filling

1 litre (35 fl oz) milk

Zest of 1 organic lemon, peeled
    off in a single strip

1 cinnamon stick

1 teaspoon vanilla sugar

200 g (7 oz) icing (confectioners')
    sugar

70 g (2½ oz) cornflour (cornstarch)

6 egg yolks

20 g (¾ oz) butter

Sugar for sprinkling

For the sponge cake

3 egg whites

1 pinch salt

75 g (2½ oz) sugar

2 teaspoons vanilla sugar

3 egg yolks

75 g (2½ oz) plain (all-purpose) flour

3 teaspoons baking powder

PREPARE THE FILLING

Bring 750 ml (26 fl oz) of the milk, the lemon zest, cinnamon stick and vanilla sugar to the boil in a saucepan, stirring. Take off the heat and leave to cool a little.

Pour the remaining milk into a tall bowl and whisk in first the icing sugar, then the cornflour and finally the egg yolks. Remove and discard the cinnamon stick and lemon zest from the cooled milk and stir in the egg yolk mixture. Transfer to a double boiler and heat over low heat, stirring constantly, until it starts to set. As soon as the cream reaches a uniform consistency, take it off the heat and whisk in the butter. Leave to cool.

BAKE THE SPONGE MIXTURE AND SHAPE INTO A ROLL

Preheat the oven to 160°C (320°F). Beat the egg whites, salt, half of the sugar and the vanilla sugar until stiff.

Whisk the egg yolks and the remaining sugar until foamy in another bowl. Very carefully fold the beaten egg whites into the egg yolk mixture. Sift the flour and baking powder on top and fold in carefully.

Spread the sponge mixture evenly on a Swiss roll tin lined with baking paper and bake for 10 minutes. Remove from the oven and transfer the sponge to a clean tea towel. Trim the edges with a knife to straighten. Roll up the sponge using the towel and leave to cool.

Once cool, carefully unroll the sponge again and spread it evenly with three-quarters of the filling, about 5 mm (¼ inch) thick. Leave the last 3–5 cm (1¼–2 inches) of the sponge uncovered. Roll the sponge up again, starting from the side with the filling all the way to the edge. Use the remaining filling to seal both ends of the roll and spread it all over the outside. Sprinkle the cake with plenty of sugar. Caramelise the sugar with a small kitchen blowtorch, as you would with a *crema catalana*.

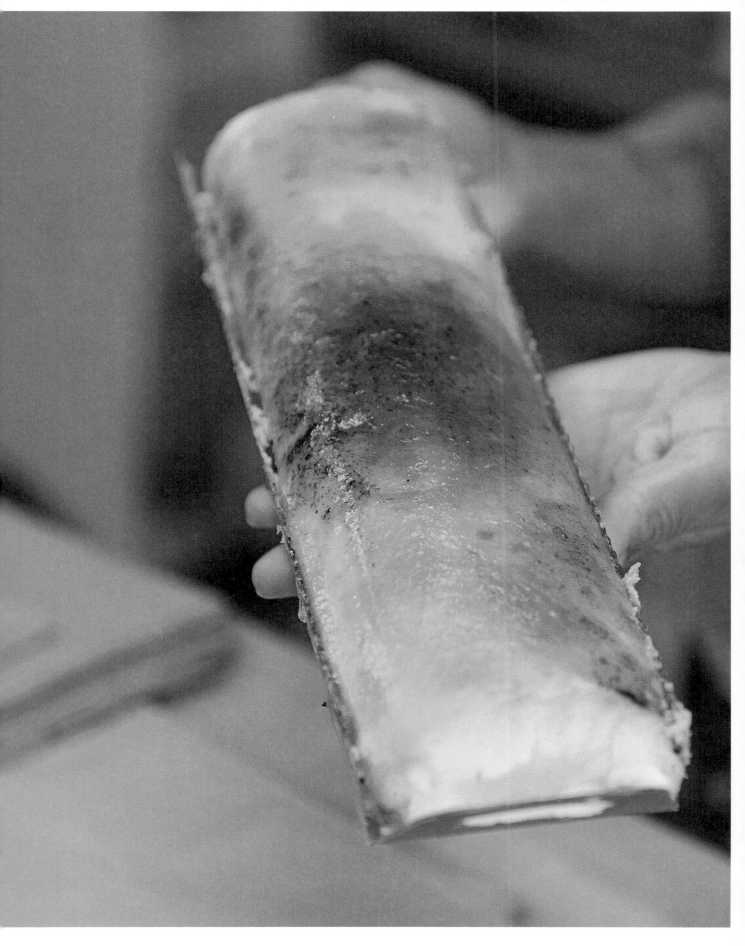

FIGUES AMB FORMATGE DE CABRA
COLL DE DAMA CON QUESO DE CABRA
GOAT'S CHEESE IN A RICE PAPER PARCEL

Personally, I don't often have desserts in restaurants, simply because I'm too full already or what's on offer is too sweet for my taste. Nevertheless, some chefs have been able to entice me to have dessert, mostly when their recipes involve a clever combination of sweet and savoury flavours, as is often the case in Spain. By the way: the best figs you can get anywhere in Catalonia are deliciously named Coll de dama, or 'Lady's neck'.

Serves 4 | **Preparation:** 15 minutes | **Cooking time:** 5 minutes

INGREDIENTS

4 figs (use Coll de dama, if
    available)
4 small sprigs rosemary
4 small round goat's cheese
    (e.g. Cabécou)
4 rice paper sheets, soaked in water
Olive oil for frying
A little balsamic vinegar

PREPARATION

Remove the stem bases from the figs and cut a slice 1 cm (½ inch) thick out of the thickest section of each fig. Finely dice the remaining fruit. Trim the soft tips off the rosemary sprigs and set aside. Pick off some leaves from the remaining sprigs, chop and combine with the diced figs in a bowl.

Stack 1 rosemary tip, 1 slice of fig and 1 goat's cheese round in the centre of each sheet of softened rice paper. Fold the rice paper in to make a small parcel.

Heat plenty of olive oil in a pan over high heat and fry the parcels, seam side down, for 2–3 minutes until golden brown, then flip over and cook the other side for another 2 minutes.

Season the diced fig and rosemary mixture to taste with balsamic vinegar and serve it with the golden brown cheese parcels.

SORBET DE PRUNES
SORBETE DE CIRUELA
PLUM SORBET

Spain is blessed with an abundance of vegetable- and fruit-growing areas.
The fertile Ebro valley produces an excellent variety of plums, among others.
In Barcelona, these are often transformed into a beautifully coloured, refreshing sorbet.

Serves 4 | **Preparation:** 10 minutes | **Cooking time:** 20 minutes | **Freezing time:** 5 hours

INGREDIENTS

7–9 large, ripe plums

3 tablespoons sugar

1 cinnamon stick, plus extra for
    garnish

1 star anise, plus extra for garnish

200 ml (7 fl oz) red wine

PREPARATION

Halve the plums and remove the stones. Quarter one plum and set aside.

Heat the sugar with 3 tablespoons water in a saucepan over medium heat. As soon as the sugar starts to brown, add the plum halves and stir well to prevent the sugar from burning. Add the large cinnamon stick and the star anise. Simmer for 4–5 minutes, then deglaze with the wine and continue to simmer until the plums are soft.

Remove the cinnamon stick and star anise. Strain the fruit purée through a sieve and sweeten to taste. Leave the mixture to cool, then transfer to an ice cream maker to churn; alternatively, freeze for a few hours in a bowl. If freezing, stir the mixture regularly, every 30 minutes if possible, to break down any ice crystals as they form.

Serve the sorbet in chilled cocktail glasses, garnished with a plum wedge, cinnamon sticks and star anise.

This sorbet also tastes great with doughnut peaches or any other sweet, aromatic fruit of your choice.

TARONJA, TARONJA I TARONJA
NARANJA, NARANJA Y NARANJA
ORANGES THREE WAYS

Oranges are fantastic fruits. Both the delicious, healthy pulp and the highly aromatic zest (without any of the white skin) are perfect for using in the kitchen. There's plenty of scope for pleasant surprises.

Serves 4 | **Preparation:** 20 minutes | **Cooking time:** 1 hour 5 minutes | **Marinating time:** 3 hours

INGREDIENTS

8 organic oranges
2–3 tablespoons sugar
50 ml (1½ fl oz) orange liqueur
    (Grand Marnier or Cointreau)

PREPARATION

Peel the zest from the oranges, keeping the strips not too short, but making them as thin as possible. Be careful to avoid any of the white skin, as it is bitter. Slice the orange zest into thin julienne strips. Add the orange zest to a saucepan of boiling water and simmer for 15–20 minutes. Strain and set aside.

Dissolve the sugar in 4 tablespoons water in a small saucepan over low heat, then add the orange zest. Simmer for 45 minutes or until all of the liquid has evaporated and the sugar starts to crystallise. Be careful not to let the sugar brown. Transfer the orange zest strips to a sheet of foil, ideally keeping the strips separate so they do not stick together. Leave to cool.

Fillet the oranges, reserving any juice. Transfer the orange fillets to a bowl and cover with the liqueur. Marinate in the refrigerator for 3 hours. Refrigerate the reserved orange juice as well.

To serve, divide the orange fillets among four glass bowls. Drizzle with the marinade and juice and garnish with the candied orange peel.

'El Xampanyet' in Barcelona's Carrer de Montcada likes to serve *xampán* al fresco in classic champagne saucers.

NÍSPEROS EN ORUJO
NÍSPEROS EN ORUJO
MEDLAR WITH ORUJO SPIRIT

Medlars are an incredibly healthy fruit that are also excellent for preserving. Preserved medlars form the basis for this delicious dessert served in Barcelona's 'Quimet & Quimet', a tapas bar steeped in Catalan tradition. Orujo is a spirit distilled from grape marc. It is similar to grappa, but higher in alcohol. Orujo is usually consumed chilled. This dessert is as simple as it is unconventional.

Serves 4 | **Preparation:** 5 minutes

INGREDIENTS

4 medlars from a jar (available
   from specialist suppliers)
Orujo (grape marc spirit)
Medlar syrup (from the jar)
Ground cinnamon

PREPARATION

Quarter the medlars and transfer the quarters to large shot glasses or cocktail glasses. Fill the glasses one-third with *orujo* and two-thirds with medlar syrup.

Pierce the medlar pieces a few times and dust them with cinnamon. Serve with a fork and spoon – done!

SORBET DE MANDARINA

SORBETE DE MANDARINA
MANDARIN SORBET

Spanish sweets and desserts are (in)famous for being just that: sweet. But there are some exceptions that are less sweet and all the more refreshing, among them this sorbet.

Serves 4 | **Preparation:** 10 minutes | **Marinating time:** 1 hour | **Chilling time:** 5 hours

INGREDIENTS

2–3 cm (¾–1¼ inch) piece fresh
    ginger
Juice of 8 sweet, aromatic organic
    mandarins
40 ml (1¼ fl oz) vodka
1 pinch ground allspice
2 mandarin slices, halved
4 sprigs mint

PREPARATION

Peel and mince the ginger. Combine with the mandarin juice in a bowl. Stir in the vodka and season with allspice.

Leave the mixture to marinate in the refrigerator for 1 hour. Strain and transfer to an ice cream maker to churn; alternatively, freeze for 4–5 hours in a bowl. If freezing, keep stirring the mixture regularly, every 30 minutes if possible, to break down any ice crystals as they form.

Serve the sorbet in chilled cocktail glasses, garnished with half a mandarin slice and a sprig of mint each.

SORBET DE SINDRÍA AMB ALFABERGA

SORBETE DE SANDÍA CON ALBAHACA
WATERMELON SORBET WITH BASIL

I love dining out, and I love culinary surprises. With some restaurants, I've come to a kind of agreement, where they'll divulge their recipe if I'm able to guess all of the ingredients by taste. It's an intriguing deal for me, through which I've managed to uncover the secrets of this summery dessert.

Serves 4 | **Preparation:** 10 minutes | **Freezing time:** 4 hours

INGREDIENTS

¼ ripe watermelon
80 g (2¾ oz) fresh basil leaves, plus some extra for garnish
Icing (confectioners') sugar
Rosewater

PREPARATION

Dice the watermelon into 2–3 cm (¾–1¼ inch) pieces. Reserve any juice and remove as many of the seeds as possible. Transfer the pieces to a bowl and freeze for 3–4 hours. Refrigerate the reserved juice.

Just before serving, sprinkle the basil leaves with plenty of icing sugar and chop very finely to make a coarse paste that shouldn't be too firm.

Quickly blend the frozen watermelon and chilled watermelon juice to a sorbet in a blender or food processor.

Divide the sorbet among chilled cocktail glasses and garnish with the basil paste. Transfer the rosewater to an atomiser and spray over the sorbet. Serve immediately, garnished with a basil leaf each.

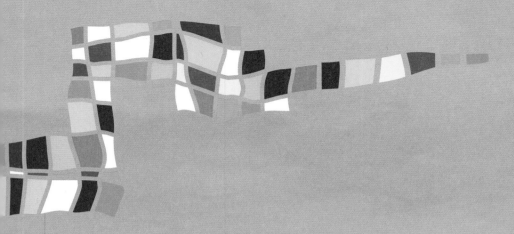

Spain is a country of wines, and Spanish wines are generally quite high in alcohol: almost all have 12% alcohol or more. Barcelona is surrounded by the vineyards of Empordá, Girona and Maresme in the north and north-west and the lush region of the Penedès in the south-west.

Spain, and Catalonia in particular, are home not only to amazing wines and some very enjoyable beers, but also to the (in)famous sangría, which is – how should one put it – very popular around Mallorcan resorts.

In Barcelona, the bars on Las Ramblas serve sangría that is so sweet it almost sticks to the palate, but properly prepared it can be truly delightful. It also has a refreshing, sparkling sibling, the *sangría de cava*, which comes from the Penedès region around Barcelona. In summer, *tinto de verano*, red wine with sparkling, sweetened mineral water, is yet another popular drink in the city's bars.

Barcelona has its very own beer, the 'Moritz', named after the local brewery's Alsatian founder. The brewery runs its own pub in the city centre, which has been refurbished and reopened and now serves refreshing beer on tap.

Spaniards love to have an after-dinner *café*, that is, a short black. Or you could have a *cortado*, which is a short black with a dash of milk, or a *carajillo*, a short black with liqueur or some kind or spirit. Any coffee is usually served together with a glass of ice cubes, especially in summer. Once the coffee has been sweetened to taste, it is poured over the ice cubes to chill and then enjoyed immediately. Other popular drinks to have after dinner are digestifs, most commonly brandy or rum, ice-cold *orujo*, a type of grape marc spirit, or *hierba*, a herb liqueur.

DRINKS

SANGRÍA

SANGRÍA
SANGRIA

If a sangría *is prepared with the right ingredients, it can be enjoyed without any fear of suffering a hangover the next day. There are literally hundreds of methods for preparing* sangría *– some of them quick, some of them slow. However, a really good* sangría *does take a little time, and this particular one is certainly a few leagues above those served in Mallorcan resorts or on Las Ramblas.*

Makes 2 litres (70 fl oz) | **Preparation:** 10 minutes | **Cooking time:** 10 minutes | **Chilling time:** 2 hours

INGREDIENTS

2 tablespoons sugar

1 small cinnamon stick

1 pinch freshly ground nutmeg

1 glass cognac or rum

1 bottle dry, young red wine,
    well chilled

Juice of 2 organic oranges

Juice of 1 organic lemon

2 peaches, diced

1 apple, diced

Halved slices of 1 organic orange

Lemon- or orange-flavoured
    sparkling mineral water

PREPARATION

Heat the sugar in 2 tablespoons water in a saucepan over medium heat, stirring, then add the cinnamon stick. Take the saucepan off the heat as soon as the liquid starts to boil. Leave to cool and add the nutmeg and cognac.

Transfer to a large jug and add the wine and the juices. Add the fruit to the liquid. If you like your *sangría* a bit sweeter, top it up with sweetened sparkling mineral water to taste. Refrigerate the *sangría* for at least 2 hours. Serve with ice cubes.

SANGRÍA DE CAVA
SANGRÍA DE CAVA
CAVA SANGRIA

A different version, sangría de cava, *makes a particularly refreshing summer drink that is just as easily prepared.* Sangría de cava *originated in the immediate surroundings of Barcelona, where sparkling cava wine is produced.*

Makes 1.2 litres (42 fl oz) | **Preparation:** 10 minutes

INGREDIENTS

1 organic orange, quartered
   and sliced
1 organic lemon, sliced
200 ml (7 fl oz) orange lemonade
200 ml (7 fl oz) lemonade
400 ml (14 fl oz) Cointreau
400 ml (14 fl oz) dry vermouth
   (Martini or Noilly Prat)
Ice cubes to taste
1 bottle cava brut, well chilled

PREPARATION

Combine the fruit, two types of lemonade, Cointreau and vermouth in a large jug. Add the ice cubes and carefully pour the cava on top, trying to preserve as much of the fizz as possible. Stir gently and serve immediately.

CAVA

If there is a single drink that is inseparably linked with Barcelona, it's cava, the typically Spanish sparkling wine. Cava is a dry sparkling wine that is generally produced from macabeu, parellada and xarel-lo grapes. In Australia, the best-known cava brands are 'Freixenet' and 'Cordoníu', but there are about 100 other vineyards that also make absolutely exquisite cava. One of my personal favourites comes from the 'Agustí Torelló' vineyard.

CREMAT
CREMAT
FLAMBÉ RUM COFFEE

Cremat is particularly popular around the beginning of summer, when people love sitting outside on the beaches until late. Cremat is always prepared fresh. It's also a popular drink served from stalls at community fairs. Cremat is a bit like a mulled wine flambé. It is generally prepared after sunset, and the flambéing process is a little celebration of its own.

Serves 4–6 | **Preparation:** 10 minutes | **Cooking time:** 25 minutes

INGREDIENTS

500 ml (17 fl oz) cachaça (spirit
   distilled from sugar cane)
500 ml (17 fl oz) brown rum
Zest of ½ an organic lemon,
   peeled off in a single strip
2 cinnamon sticks
5 coffee beans
5 tablespoons sugar
250 ml (9 fl oz) black coffee

PREPARATION

Add the cachaça, rum, lemon zest, cinnamon sticks and coffee beans to a large saucepan. Stir in the sugar until dissolved and heat the mixture over medium heat.

Remove a small amount of the liquid with a ladle. Light the liquid in the ladle and carefully return the burning alcohol to the saucepan to allow the flames to spread across the whole surface.

Leave to burn for a little while, while you prepare the coffee. Keep stirring to ensure that the alcohol burns down slowly. Once the flames get weaker after 15–20 minutes, stir in the coffee and serve in coffee cups.

MOJITO SIN ALCOHOL
MOJITO SIN ALCOHOL
VIRGIN MOJITO

What would a day on Barcelona's beaches be without ending it over a decent cocktail or two? However, sometimes life throws a spanner in the works in the form of random breath testing stations on your way home. Not to worry, though – people in Barcelona are very ingenious, and some beach bars serve delectable virgin mojitos that are almost indistinguishable from their not-so-virtuous cousins. Ginger is added for extra spice and to impart a flavour similar to alcohol. If you still get pulled over by the police, maybe it's the mojitos from the previous night that are still lingering...

Serves 4–6 | **Preparation:** 10 minutes | **Chilling time:** 30 minutes

INGREDIENTS

6–8 organic limes
Fine brown sugar to taste
1 medium-sized piece of fresh
 ginger, thinly sliced
1 handful of mint leaves, torn
Ice cubes
750 ml (26 fl oz) chilled mineral
 water

PREPARATION

Slice 1 lime and set aside. Cut the remaining limes into 8 wedges each. Add the brown sugar and pound in a mortar and pestle to squeeze out the juice. Transfer the ginger into a glass carafe and add the sugar and lime juice mixture. Chill for 30 minutes.

Remove the carafe from the refrigerator and add the mint leaves, slices of lime and ice cubes. Top with the mineral water, stir and serve.

Where, if not here? In Barcelona, there's always time and a relaxing place for a coffee.

Olive oil is an absolute must in Barcelonian cuisine, as in all
Spanish cooking. When I say olive oil, I always mean cold-pressed
oil of the highest quality. My favourite is the oil pressed from the
tiny arbequina olives, which are very typically Catalan, although
they were only introduced to Catalonia from the Middle East in
the 17th century. Arbequinas produce a richly aromatic and fruity
oil. For me, the best olive oils come from the region around Lleida
and the counties of Siurana near Tarragona and Garrotxa north
of Barcelona. For basic frying and deep-frying, it's perfectly fine
to use sunflower oil or peanut oil, though.

Barcelonian cuisine works with a number of very special
ingredients. A typical example would be a *picada*, which forms
an essential part of many different recipes and is used to thicken
liquids and to enhance the natural flavour and aroma of foods.
A *picada* usually consists of dry bread, hazelnuts, almonds, flat-leaf
(Italian) parsley and garlic, but there are endless variations of this
basic recipe. Catalan cooking also relies extensively on *ñora* or
nyora peppers. These plum-sized, round, reddish-black dried
peppers have a mildly spicy flavour and appear again and again
in Catalan recipes, including in a local take on paella. They also
form an essential part of *romesco* sauce (see page 261) and all of
its variations. As these peppers impart a lovely golden-red hue to
foods, they are also used as a substitute for saffron. Sourcing *nyora*
peppers may be a bit of a challenge – alternatively use other mildly
spicy peppers or chillies or mildly spicy chilli powder for heat and
flavour or saffron for colour.

Classics of Spanish and Catalan cooking such as *all i oli* and
samfaina are, of course, a must in a lot of the recipes in this book.
However, their use is by no means limited to this regional cuisine,
and they complement an endless number of dishes.